VICTORIAN PLYMOUTH

CW00820184

CHRIS ROBINSON

British Library Cataloguing in Publication Data

Chris Robinson
Victorian Plymouth
A Tour Around the Three Towns and Surrounding Neighbourhood
A catalogue record for this book is available from the British Library
ISBN 978-0-9934812-2-2

Compiled and illustrated by Chris Robinson
Layout Chris Robinson
© Chris Robinson 2016

First published 2016

Also available in this series:
Plymouth's Great War: The Three Towns United in Conflict
Plymouth in the Twenties & Thirties
It Came To Our Door
Plymouth in the Forties & Fifties
Plymouth in the Fifties & Sixties
Plymouth in the Seventies

All rights reserved. No part of this publication may be reproduced
stored in a retrieval system or transmitted, in any form or by any other means,
electronic, mechanical, photocopying, recording or otherwise,
without the prior permission of Pen & Ink (Publishing).

Published by
Pen & Ink Publishing
34 New Street, Barbican
Plymouth PL1 2NA
Tel: 01752 228120 /705337
www.chrisrobinson.co.uk

Printed and bound in Great Britain by
Latimer Trend & Company Ltd
Estover Close
Plymouth PL6 7PL

CONTENTS

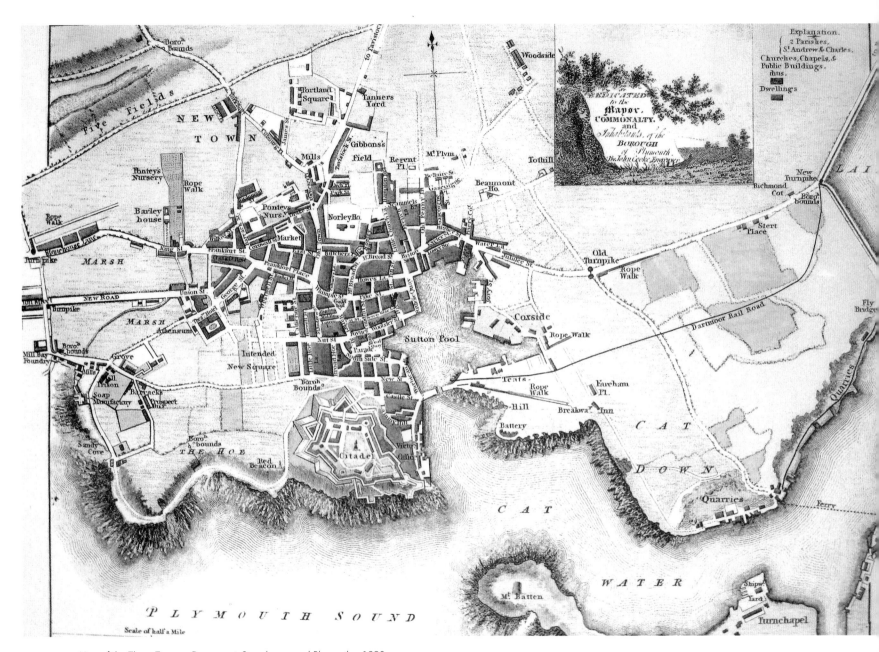

Map of the Three Towns – Devonport, Stonehouse and Plymouth c.1820.

INTRODUCTION

Ever since finding a copy of WHK Wright's *Illustrated Handbook to Plymouth, Stonehouse & Devonport*, almost a 100 years after it was first published in 1879, I have thought how wonderful it would have been if it had been really well illustrated, rather than just relying on the odd sketch every few pages. To a certain extent this book goes part of the way towards achieving that.

However, I was also mindful of the fact that Wright was describing a rapidly changing Plymouth and that actually Plymouth quite possibly changed more in the Victorian era than it has done at any other time in the last 1,000 years, notwithstanding the devastating fourteenth-century Breton Raids and the calamitous bombing raids of the Second World War.

Essentially the changes in the late nineteenth century were the product of a peaceful and dramatic population increase, but, in some respects, those changes were just as destructive, especially to the historic fabric of the town.

Plymouth's first school (established in 1561 and built in 1615) was pulled down to make way for a new Guildhall, as was the town's first hospital (1630).

Palace Court, where Catherine of Aragon had been so royally entertained in 1501, was demolished and replaced by a Board School, thatched buildings in Old Town Street were replaced and then demolished to allow the street to be widened, electricity cables to be laid and the electric tram to be accommodated.

A large section of Ebrington Street was also felled, ancient buildings in Bedford Street were removed — the Island and the Globe among them. Elsewhere in How Street and Looe Street, two of the town's oldest thoroughfares, dozens of overcrowded old buildings were reduced to rubble in the name of slum clearance and the town's first Municipal Dwellings took their place.

Meanwhile, and at this point it's worth taking a good look at the map opposite, we must remember that the population of Plymouth, which expanded sixfold during the century, had, by 1820, not massively changed from the Plymouth that the Pilgrim Fathers would have seen 200 years earlier.

The signs were there though: see the area marked 'New Town' in the top left-hand corner and note the green space that still separated it from the Old Town. Drake would still have found much of this familiar — he may have been amazed by the Citadel, which represented a huge expansion of his 1590s fort by Fisher's Nose, and he would have been intrigued by John Foulston's new Theatre Royal — a building many deemed to be too far out of town to be successful. Fundamentally, though the town occupied much the same footprint as it had when our former local hero, Sir Francis Drake — Mayor, MP and land-owner (he held the deeds to over 30 properties in the town) — walked these streets.

Within one lifetime, however, all that had changed. The Industrial Revolution brought with it a cultural revolution, a population boom and a seismic shift in working practices — when Queen Victoria came to the throne it was estimated that agriculture accounted for around a quarter of the workforce, by 1900 it was less than half that. But this book is not intended to address the human or social side of Plymouth in Victorian times, rather it is an attempt to visually depict just how those changes impacted on the local landscape and to accompany those images with contmeporary accounts — from newspapers, magazines and books.

The book represents an attempt to do what the title suggests, take the reader on a tour of the Three Towns and Surrounding Neighbourhood from the perspective of someone writing at the end of the Nineteenth Century. To that end I have written connecting text in the present tense, so it is up to the individual to consider what happened next. I have tried to avoid hindsight, and indeed, looking into the future. Hopefully this will give you more of a Victorian perspective on the Plymouth before 1900.

It is precisely because of this approach that I have also avoided tackling topics like the Crimean War, the Zulu Wars and the Boer War. This, quite literally, is a look at the area as your, and my, ancestors would have seen it: it aims to give an idea of what that generation would have made of a situation where the map of Plymouth changed from the one we see opposite to the one we see overleaf.

ILLUSTRATED

HANDBOOK

TO

PLYMOUTH,

STONEHOUSE & DEVONPORT,

With a New Map.

BY

W. H. K. WRIGHT,

PUBLIC LIBRARIAN.
FELLOW OF THE ROYAL HISTORICAL SOCIETY.
MEMBER OF THE PLYMOUTH INSTITUTION.
AUTHOR OF "THE VISITORS' GUIDE TO MOUNT EDGCUMBE."
"THE SPANISH ARMADA," A DESCRIPTIVE HISTORICAL POEM, ETC.

NEW AND ENLARGED EDITION.

PLYMOUTH:
W. H. LUKE, BEDFORD STREET.

Here, at the end of the century, we see that Plymouth is no longer Three separate Towns, other than in name. The boundaries have all been pushed out to meet each other

The growth of Stonehouse has been constrained by its geography, and its bigger neighbours, meanwhile Plymouth and Devonport are both expanding northwards at a staggering rate, swallowing up green fields at an unprecedented pace — a pace perhaps only matched locally by the post-war effort to rehouse those displaced by the Blitz.

Of course, other aspects of life tackled vicariously through the pages of this book include the great changes in transport: the arrival of the train and the tram and the impact of gas, steam and electricity.

Entertainment, leisure, and education also have their place here as do work, commerce, and industry. But essentially this is a large collection of nineteenth century images, mostly taken between 1850 and 1900 — although, as most of them are not dated, there are bound to be a few Edwardian and other interlopers — that is designed to provide an insight into an area before the age of the car, the bus and the aeroplane; before the era of domestic electrical supplies and wireless communication.

Newspapers there were, and two of the most enduring publications to serve the area, the *Western Morning News* and the *Evening Herald*, both started life during this period. Frequently, however, local stories made it into other titles around the country and at the end of the book in the acknowledgements you will find a key to quotes contained in the book, not only from newspapers, but from other publications too.

Local writers Whitfeld, Worth and Wright are the most regularly called upon for a quote, particularly WHK Wright.

Born in December 1845, William Wright was in his early 30s when he produced the Handbook that so much of this present tome is based upon. He also authored the *Streets of Old Plymouth*, produced with the artist Charles Eldred in 1901 as well as a number of other magazine and periodical pieces. For many years he served as Borough Librarian, living in Headland House, at the top of North Hill with his wife Jeannette.

I wonder what they'd make of Plymouth today ... and of this book. I'd like to think it's the sort of volume he would like to have put together himself — Victorian Plymouth as the Victorians saw it and described it.

Chris Robinson *October 2016*

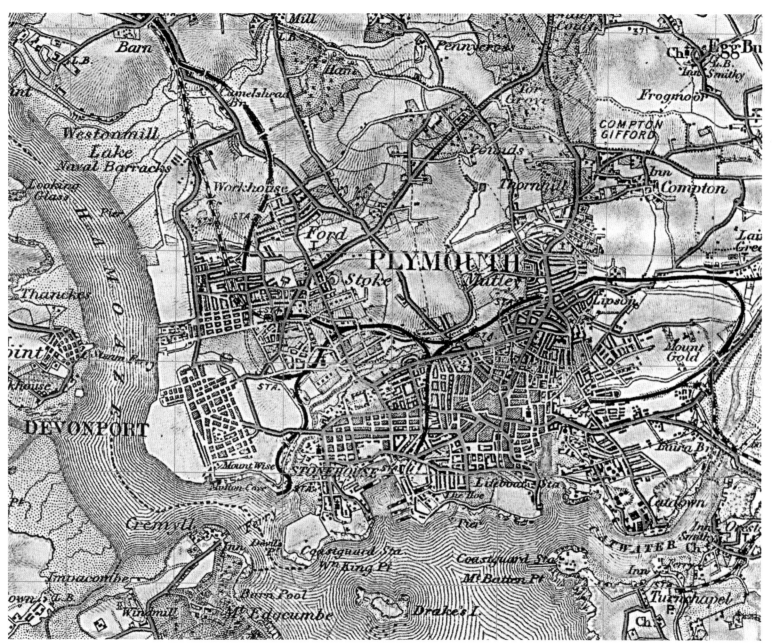

Map of the Three Towns – Devonport, Stonehouse and Plymouth c.1901.

7

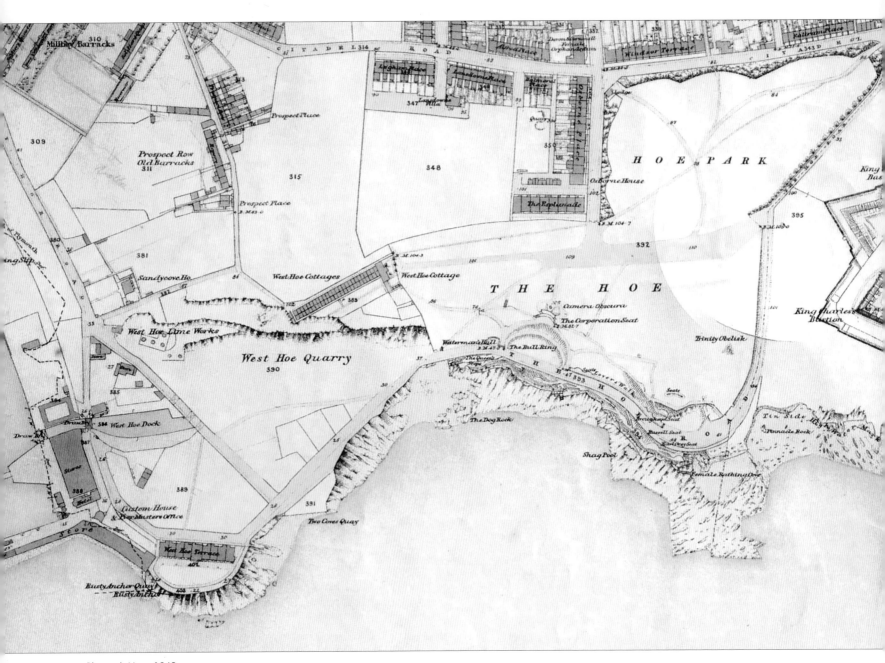

Plymouth Hoe c1868

PLYMOUTH HOE

'The Hoe is a commanding eminence which bounds the inward or northern line of Plymouth Sound and extends from Millbay to the Citadel. Considerable improvements have been made of late years, by the formation of carriage-drives and commodious walks, with seats at due intervals, forming a public promenade — an appropriation which, from the salubrity and pleasantness of this fine elevation, has been most beneficial to the inhabitants. It has just been styled 'the lungs of Plymouth' for here the inhabitants of all grades, resort for air and exercise.

'With a view to the further improvement of this delightful place the Town Council of Plymouth, in 1847, effected an arrangement with the Board of Ordnance, and obtained a lease of the field called the Governor's Meadow, on the northeast side of the Hoe. The fence separating the two has been removed, and two beautiful walks made through it.

'At the head of Lockyer Street a neat lodge has been built, and ornamental shrubs planted on the northern and western sides of the ground: and it now bears the appellation of Hoe Park.' (TSH 1851)

Above: *The Hoe Lodge in May 1848, 34-year-old EJ Kessel was appointed as the Hoe Constable. During the summer months he was expected to be constantly on duty supervising the Hoe and Governor's Field. The following year it was decreed that games were to be allowed in the Governor's Field, but not on the Hoe itself. Kessel, who lived in the lodge, held the post until 1877, when he retired with a pension of 16 shillings a week.*

'The Hoe proper consists of a series of grassy slopes, surrounded by a spacious promenade, and intersected by numerous paths leading to the lower grounds. At the foot of this eminence is a drive, which was formed in the year 1817 by the poor of the town, the cost being defrayed by public subscription. Connected with this road are paths leading to the rocks and landing steps at the water's edge.

'The promenade at the summit of the Hoe is nearly half-a-mile in length, extending from the Citadel on the east to the West Hoe Quarries on the west.

Above: A panorama of the Hoe from around 1870 showing the early 1850s developments of West Hoe Terrace (Grand Parade), West Hoe Cottages and even earlier 1840s-built Esplanade.

'The Park is chiefly used by the youths of the town for the purposes of recreation. Here they congregate in large numbers to indulge in the good old English game of cricket. The several military bands perform here at stated times each week; a handsome and commodious stand having recently been erected for their accommodation at the expense of the town. There are few more pleasant methods of spending a spare hour than by taking a saunter on the Hoe on a fine summer afternoon.

'The inspiriting influence of the music, as performed by a band of musicians — the Royal Marines — scarcely inferior to any in the kingdom; the liveliness of the scene caused by the assemblage of hundreds of persons of both sexes and from amongst the most fashionable classes of society; the gay dresses of the ladies, who here delight to display all the adornments which nature and fashion combined have bestowed upon them; those and many other attractions, contribute (with the all powerful aid of a bright sun, a clear sky, and a freshening breeze) a sense of pleasurable excitement, which is quite invigorating after the fatigues of business life, imparting a new zest with which to enter upon a fresh round of duties.

'The Hoe was formerly used for military display, but of late years these have been held on more commodious grounds nearer to the barracks, namely, at the Brickfields, Devonport.

'Near the eastern end of the grassy lawn is a peculiar triangular structure. This object serves as a landmark for vessels at sea. *(Wright 1879)*

Top left: Enjoying the sun on a summer day. Top right: The Camera Obscura sits far left with the Corporation Seat below it and the Trinity Obelisk to the right. Right: A wider view of the scene with the West Hoe Quarry in the foreground.

'Near the centre of the Promenade is a small octagonal building, called the Camera Obscura, where, for a small charge, the panorama of the surrounding scenery may be witnessed in miniature. Outside is a raised platform and a flagstaff, around which are wont to congregate some of the semi-nautical and male gossips of the neighbourhood. Here they meet to discuss some popular topic of the day, or talk over some more active period of their lives.

'Immediately below the Camera, and approachable by a flight of steps, is a commodious seat, which is usually appropriated by another and not less interesting class of men.

'Here were wont to assemble (with that regularity for which servicemen are so famous), some of those veterans, who in their youth, sailed with Nelson to victory at Trafalgar; fought under Wellington at Waterloo — could give a graphic account of the Battle of the Nile, or trod country after country during the Peninsular War — men, whose early recollections are connected with some of the most stirring events of our country's history, and who loved to tell of those days and deeds which made England famous. But these veterans are, alas, almost extinct, and their places are occupied, perchance, by those who were with Raglan in the Crimea, with Havelock at Lucknow, Napier in Abyssinia, or Wolseley at Coommassie.

'In front of this seat is the remnant of what would once have been an amphitheatre — a series of grassy galleries, with a wide arena beneath — still called the Bull Ring. To the right is a path which leads to the pebbly beach, while other paths conduct to the rocks and landing steps.

'But if we essay to engage one of the numerous watermen's boats in waiting, we must perforce, clamber over rocks and slippery steps in order to reach it, much, I fear, to the annoyance and discomfort of our lady friends, who do not at all times care to travel so rough a road in search of pleasure; for pleasure there is to be had indeed, in spite of all difficulties, whether it be a sober pull close in shore, or a spirited sail to the Breakwater and back, a distance of about six miles.

'It is hoped, however, that this drawback to pleasure and convenience may not much longer exist: a scheme being now before the public for the erection of a Promenade Pier.' *(Wright 1879)*

Top and middle: *The Camera Obscura.*
Bottom: *Looking up to the Camera and the Corporation Seat.*

A mile long and 22 yards wide (at the top), John Rennie's Breakwater was one of the constructional wonders of the world when completed at the entrance to Plymouth Sound in 1844. 'It has at one end a Lighthouse which visitors are permitted to inspect, and at the other end a Cage, capable of holding nine persons, which visitors may enter, if they have the courage to do so.' (AAGtoTTT 1881)

In 1881 Chatty Joe recorded that 'the building of the new Promenade Pier has commenced (as of January 1880), but when it will be finished we cannot say. One result of its completion we hope will be the general lighting of the Hoe either by limelight or gaslight and we shall feel a debt of gratitude to the Pier Company in bringing about a result that ought to have been accomplished years ago.'

On 29 May, three years later, the Pier was opened and the man behind the scheme, 34-year-old Edward Lancaster, was warmly congratulated:

'When some six or seven years ago Mr Lancaster looked for the first time on the grand panoramic sweep of scenery commanded from the historic promenade — the Hoe — he felt that, much as Nature had done for Plymouth, the people of Plymouth had still something to do for themselves. To Mr Lancaster it seemed that one thing was needful; that one thing he set himself to obtain with an energy and a faith which have never forsaken him, and then had the pleasure of witnessing the consummation of his hope and desires yesterday, when the Promenade Pier, which he has been the chief means of bringing into existence, was formally opened in the presence of about thirty thousand people, about one-third of whom were accommodated on the Pier itself. The weather was splendid.' (WDM 30.5.1884)

'Mr Lancaster — well known for his valuable public services to the town of his adoption — prepared, in the year 1880, a paper with the title *Plymouth a Holiday Centre*: 'From my first acquaintance with Plymouth, I was deeply impressed with the idea that it might be made a very attractive Holiday Centre, and from that day I have — in becoming more acquainted with the beauties of the neighbourhood — been surprised that the great variety of magnificent scenery, without any concerted action on the part of the inhabitants in this respect, has not secured for Plymouth a greater number of visitors.

Top: *The original plan for the Pier with a walkway from the Hoe Promenade.* Middle: *The Pier takes shape.* Bottom: *Ready to open but without the proposed Concert Pavilion.*

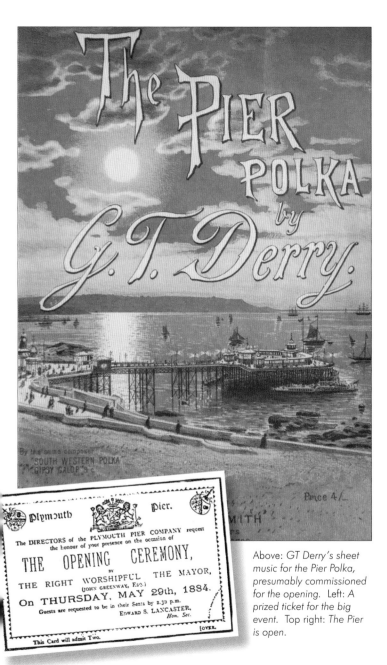

Left: Plymouth's new Pier. Right: Edward Lancaster who ran the Victoria Clothing Company in Phoenix Street, employing at one time, hundreds of hands.

Above: GT Derry's sheet music for the Pier Polka, presumably commissioned for the opening. Left: A prized ticket for the big event. Top right: The Pier is open.

'Plymouth,' said Lancaster, 'occupies the extreme south-west corner of Devon, and from its natural position in respect of the two counties, has become the Metropolis of the West, and being situated on a singularly charming part of the English coast, at the mouth of one of England's grandest rivers, possessing one of the safest and finest harbours in the world, and surrounded as it is with every possible variety of scenery, offers all the advantages necessary for a "Holiday Centre".'

Mr Lancaster made it his business to take counsel with Messrs. Cook and Son, the tourist agents, and from them, or rather their representative, gleaned some valuable information. 'My chief aim was to find in what light Plymouth was looked upon in respect of a "Holiday Centre," and to find if any obstacles were in the way, such as adverse railway arrangements, militating against the success of Plymouth, in which case I felt sure our Chamber of Commerce would readily take action and seek their removal.

'I also asked if, in his opinion, the distance from London was any great drawback. Mr Howe, Messrs. Cook's representative, said he considered the railway facilities were exceptionally good, seeing that visitors could reach Plymouth from London in five minutes less than six hours, while the quickest train to Scarborough, which is fifteen miles nearer the metropolis, occupies the same time on the journey, and both by Great Western and South Western Railways, the journey was accomplished by other trains in seven hours. With regard to the distance from London this was not an object with tourists bent on seeing any particular part, and in confirmation, he quoted an important and extraordinary fact, that of all the tickets issued by their firm for the West of England district, by far the larger number is issued from the Birmingham office, for inhabitants of that town and all points north of this.

Top: A paddle steamer sits at the landing stage on the west side of the Pier, late 1880s.
Bottom: Again late 1880s, the Camera Obscura still in place, and work yet to begin on the Pavilion at the end of the Pier. The iron paddle steamer Eleanor is from the Saltash Steam Boat Company and is heading towards West Hoe Pier, a rival provider.

'He further explained that in 1874, Cook & Son, being desirous of opening up the West of England to visitors by means of their tours, visited the principal towns from Torquay to Penzance, soliciting subscriptions from the leading tradesmen and inhabitants of this part, for a pamphlet which they produced, giving a short and concise description of the points of interest *en route* which contains lithographs of several parts of Torquay, Plymouth, Falmouth and Penzance. Mr Howe here describes Plymouth *"as especially interesting as a tourist resort, as it is important and rich in historical associations"*.

'In further conversation, Messrs. Cook's representative assured me that, in his opinion, there was no spot in the United Kingdom so naturally suited for a "Holiday Centre," but, he added, *"There seems to be no disposition on the part of the inhabitants to move in the matter."'*

One of the first to publicly promote tourism in the area, if not the founding father of the initiative, Edward Lancaster perhaps has done more than anyone to put Plymouth on the map.

The Promenade Pier was certainly the grandest gesture to date in a bid to attract tourism and Lancaster not only actively promoted the scheme, but spent five years as secretary of the body that championed its development.

The architect for the scheme was the celebrated engineer-cum-architect Eugenius Birch. As a boy, Birch had drawn up a design for a railway carriage where the wheels were placed under the passenger carriage not at the side, like a horse-drawn carriage. The London & Greenwich Company, seeing that this would create more space for passengers, adopted the design. Later he worked on a number of railway and other projects, but it was as a seaside architect of piers that he made his name. Margate was his first, West Brighton his most famous and Plymouth his last — sadly he died in January 1884, just months before it opened.

Anticipating demand for its use as a landing-point, the Plymouth Promenade Pier & Steam Packet Company Limited was set up in 1883. Landing steps and moorings were provided on either side of the Pier and a penny toll was charged for each passenger embarking or disembarking. Initially only the Oreston & Turnchapel Steamboat Co Ltd took up the opportunity to run trips from the Pier, but 'after only two Wednesdays the Promenade Pier owners shut us out.'

Henceforth the Pier owners granted a monopoly to AE Rowe in August 1884. Curiously, though, Rowe chose to re-engage the Oreston & Turnchapel steamers.

The operation of the pleasure-steamer trade was not the only area of controversy surrounding the Pier at this time, however, as an application to erect a covered pavilion early the following year divided local opinion. Those against were principally concerned that their view of the Sound would be compromised by such an addition. Those in favour included the man who, in a few years time, as a member of the Corporation, would advocate the removal of the Camera Obscura — local builder, Thomas Jinkin.

In a letter to the *Western Morning News* in May 1885, he wrote: 'Sir, It is gratifying to me, and I am quite sure to many thousands of my fellow townsmen, and I may add of the Three Towns and neighbourhood, that there is an application to be made to the Council to erect a form of covering on the pier.

'After the very large number that visited the Pier last summer I am quite sure that some portion should be covered in. Supposing two or three thousand persons being present at one time, the present shelter or wind screen would not likely accommodate one quarter of the number that would be likely to assemble there.

'I should like to draw your attention to, and I doubt not but that you have been at Portsmouth, and would have visited the South Pier, as I have myself, where there is a beautiful covering and every comfort that can be desired.

'As regards the obstruction of the view from the top of the Hoe, I am quite sure that quite 90 per cent of the people that walk on the Hoe would not object to its erection. Admitting there is a little of the through sight that would be taken, should there not be a little consideration for a company that will build such a handsome and convenient place for our comfort?' Jinkin then added: 'I do hope the day is not far distant when the present tram road that is now lying idle will become the property of the present Pier Company; and then to be able to issue through tickets from Mannamead all along the lane on to the Pier will be a great boon to the public.'

A few days later, writing from Founder's Court, London, the Chairman of the Pier Company, Albert Grant, added his weight to the debate: 'My own distinct belief is that what we propose putting up will not be an obstruction, but on the contrary will be a distinct improvement to the prospect, and, as I told Mr Derry when I met him at the railway, "a thing of beauty," and as he added then, "a joy forever," which is precisely what I want it to be.'

Top: *The Pier as first constructed without the Pavilion.* Below: *An early view with the completed structure. The application to construct a Pavilion at the end of the Pier initially met with resistance, principally on the grounds that it would obstruct the view of Drake's Island. Those fears were to prove largely unfounded.*

Baron Albert Grant, as he was styled, courtesy of an Italian title (that allegedly he had purchased from Victor Emmanuel II), had, as chairman of the pier directors, overseen the raising of the £45,000 required to fund the construction. Most, if not all of this, allegedly raised outside Plymouth.

Grant, born Abraham Gottheimer, was an interesting fellow who specialised in establishing companies that were wont to fail at the shareholders expense. Twice elected MP for Kidderminster, on the second occasion, in 1874, he was unseated within months following an election expenses scandal.

From 1876 onwards he was dogged by creditors pursuing him in the Courts and in 1885 found himself in the bankruptcy courts — not for the first time — following the collapse of a bank he had set up seven years earlier.

Unsurprisingly therefore 'the construction of the Pier was a story of "fortunes and misfortunes, successes and failures. When the Pier's finished" had become synonymous in Plymouth with "When the Halfpenny Gate's abolished."

'The first contract for the construction work was undertaken by Messrs Laidlaw, Sons, & Caine, of Glasgow, and ultimately (in November 1882) passed into the hands of Mr CE Daniel of London.' (*WMN May 1884*).

In 1886 Thomas Martin agreed a three-year rental of the pier (somewhere between £800 and £1,000) and in September 1887 it was sold at auction to Walter Kay, a Plymouth fish merchant.

Five years later the Pier was taken over by a 'powerful London syndicate' and the completion of the structure came with the opening of the Pavilion.

'Capable of accommodating 5,000 people, the handsome pavilion was furnished with a boxwood floor to render it more suitable for dancing and roller skating.

'In the summer it is largely used for vocal and instrumental concerts; in the winter for balls, skating and other amusements of a sociable character. An external gallery extends to the sides of the pier, affording an elevated view and protection from the wind and rain to those below. This gallery has materially facilitated the provision of refreshments and other stuffs, which otherwise would have encroached upon the space available for concerts and other purposes with the hall of the pavilion proper.' (*NDJ June 1899*)

Opposite page: The completed Pier and Drake's Island.
Right: Three views of the horse tram servicing Plymouth Pier.

Above: *The interior of the Pavilion Pier opened in 1891.*
Left: *An 1874 cartoon from Vanity Fair of Baron Albert Grant (aka Abraham Gottheimer) an infamous company promoter, who was born in Dublin in 1831, the son of an impecunious Jewish pedlar from Central Europe. Educated in London and Paris, as Albert Grant he started work as a clerk and soon afterwards as a wine salesman.*
In his late twenties he established the first of a number of companies, most of which were ultimately unsuccessful, mainly in Britain, but also overseas.
Chairman of the Plymouth Pier Company for a number of years, he was present at the opening in 1884. A few days before his death, in 1899, he was served with a third and final receiving order. His last few years were spent in relative poverty.

Overall the pier is supported by 140 iron columns, only 10 or so of which had been erected in the first two years of construction: 'It is 420 feet in length. The width at the entrance is 130 feet, and this narrows to a causeway 60 feet wide, which again extends at its seaward extremity to a spacious promenade 190 feet across.

'The entrance from Hoe Road presents an exceedingly effective appearance; the necessary structures are light and elegant in design, and while they necessarily somewhat impede the view from the road they are calculated to give as little offence as possible to the eyes of those who think nature unadorned, adorned the most.

'The passage ways leading to the turnstiles are laid with Minton's encaustic tiles, and the central building — 40 feet long and 16 feet wide it is devoted to the purposes of a tea and luncheon room.

'On either side of the luncheon room is an octagonal toll house commanding four turnstiles, while on either hand is a gate for the admission of Bath chairs.

'The bases of the toll houses are inlaid with ornamental tiles in keeping with the passages, and the roofs are elaborately decorated with ironwork. Above the central building there is a clock tower.

'Starting from the shore end of the Pier the causeway lies on a gentle slope and terminates in six semi-circular wooden steps. At the head of the steps on either hand is a small house similar in design to the toll houses — one a cabinet des femmes and the other a gentleman's lavatory. These offices are in the charge of a female and male attendant respectively.

'The Pier is artificially lighted by 18 electrical arc lamps of 2,000 candle power each and all the rooms are fitted with Lane-Fox incandescent lamps. Below the turnstiles and toll houses is a vaulted chamber which will be used as stores and as a receptacle for the 16-horse-power gas engine by which the motive power for the electric light is to be supplied.' *(WMN May 1884)*

It is the first public building in Plymouth to be lit by electricity.

'The "deck" of the Pier is of 2½-inch pitch pine planks smoothly laid and easy to traverse.' *(ibid)*

Initially at least the catering for the refreshment rooms was entrusted to the baker and confectioner Henry Matthews, while JH Mortimer (formerly at the King's Arms in Ivybridge) became the first lessee of the Pavilion Pier in 1891.

Plymouth Pier.

Promotional material for the Pier from 1891.

By the end of the Nineteenth Century the Pier had become a firm favourite and something of a financial success:

'Those who propose to spend their coming holidays at Plymouth will find on arrival at the port that the pier has recently been entirely overhauled and redecorated, and that the various attractions which the erection offers to those who prefer to "lounge life's lazy round away" have been materially added to. It would be difficult to imagine Plymouth without its pier now.

'Certainly if it were removed one of the most noteworthy features of interest would disappear. Fortunately there is no probability of anything of this kind happening. The Plymouth Pier and Promenade Company finds its enterprise too productive of profit to abandon it, and, blow rude Boreas never so blusterously, the iron piles originally laid by Mr Fry, the well-known diver, may be relied upon to sustain their burden with ease and proper care.

'Mr Fry, who has just been below water for a visit of inspection, reports the columns to be in a first-class state of repair, and Mr Dawney, of London Bridge, who went down not long ago for the purpose of inspecting it, reports that the portion of the structure above the sea level is in excellent condition.

'On every hand there are the activity and panoramic variety which the evolutions of the numerous pleasure yachts always in the Sound, the warships, and the torpedo boats perpetually afford.

'An afternoon spent on the pier is distinctly restful to the nerves; but the quietude in no way partakes of the character of that dull monotony which is as injurious as feverish strain.

'That this place of resort is becoming more and more popular under the new and energetic management is evidenced in an indisputable fashion by the continued increase in visitors, and in the consequent revenue.

'Last Easter Monday over 10,000 people patronised the pier, while on Whit Monday the attendance was 11,000. The receipts for the latter day amounted to £117, as against £66 for the same day last year. Again on the Queen's Birthday the figures were £44, compared with £9 last year. These increases do not appear to be exceptional on account of weather conditions or other special reasons, as the takings exhibit a steady increase throughout the whole year. The total receipts to Monday, May 24, were £1,648 17s 8d. compared with £1,434 16s 10d. for the preceding year.

'The Pier is visited by the inhabitants of Plymouth, Devonport, and Stonehouse, as well as the large number of persons who temporarily come into these towns, which for all practical purposes are one, the population being over 200,000.'

'Moreover, the recent adjustment of the Great Western Railway Company's gauge has already resulted in a large increase in the number of excursionists from the North and Midlands. Shares of pier companies soundly organised and carrying on operations at popular seaside resorts are generally admitted to offer a fair opportunity for investors who like a larger return than 2½ per cent on their money. The last dividends of four such companies were at the following rates per cent: Brighton West Pier Company 13; Margate Pier and Harbour Company (prior to the damage caused by the storm of November 1897) 9; Hasting Pier Company 7½; and Blackpool Pier Company 10, with a bonus of 2. At 13-16 Plymouth Pier preference shares are a sound investment, and at 7/8ths the ordinary are something more than a promising speculation.' (NDJ June 1899)

Top: The now toll-free steamer service. Left: Steamers at the steps and a hand-cart selling ice-cream at the entrance. Right: Refreshment rooms at the end of the Pier.

The Jubilee fountain in the Bull Ring.

Directly opposite the Pier head, in 1887, Alderman King offered to provide a fountain to be erected in the Bull Ring.

Speaking at the Council meeting on 4 May that year — the Queen's Jubilee Year — Mr Pitts moved that the offer be accepted with thanks. 'Mr E James seconded the motion, and, on the suggestion of Mr Alderman Harris, there was added to it an expression of sympathy with Mr King in his illness. The motion was unanimously agreed to. Mr Pethick said he understood Mrs Mortimer Collier was quite ready to plant the Bull Ring with shrubs. Mr Pitts said he was afraid that at present that would be a waste of money.' *(WMN May 1887)*

The Bull Ring at that time was an area that regularly saw a relatively heavy footfall.

'A meeting of the Council of the County Borough of Plymouth was held yesterday [Wednesday 12 June 1889], with Mr AS Harris presiding in the absence of the Mayor. The Hoe and Recreation Ground Committee recommended that the Camera Obscura on the Hoe be taken down forthwith. This was proposed by Mr T Jinkin, seconded by Mr G Browne and agreed to.' *(WMN)*

The Camera Obscura was run by Miss Sampson, who together with her father had held the lease of the site for nearly 50 years. Its earliest incarnation, dating from the 1830s, was blown away three times prior to 1840. Supported substantially by advertising revenue, 72-year-old Miss Sampson was awarded eight shillings a week for life on surrender of the lease.

In 1891, coinciding with the completion of the Pier — and the refusal to allow a walkway to be constructed from the top of the Hoe on to the Pier — it was proposed that a shelter be erected above the Bull Ring at a likely cost of £583.

A handsome, three-tiered structure was erected, using, it is said, a number of granite Tuscan columns from the old market.

The Bull Ring remained for the time being, but the following year users of the area held a mass meeting here complaining that their rights and privileges had been compromised by the railings that had been erected there.

Then, in May 1894, at Plymouth Police Court, William Charles Salter was summoned for having delivered a public address in the Bull Ring the previous May, contrary to by-laws.

'The Town Clerk, Mr JH Ellis, said the information was laid under by-law 25 of the series of by-laws adopted by the Town Council in

1888 (and passed in 1892) for the better regulation of the Hoe, which provided that addresses could not be delivered there without the consent of the Urban Sanitary Authority.' *(WMN May 1894)*

'Primarily,' Mr Ellis continued, 'the Hoe was a recreation ground, not a place for business, or for meeting; yet the Council held themselves free to grant permission for it to be used for religious services and public addresses if they thought fit.

'W Gasking, Superintendent of Police, deposed to seeing the defendant in company with Messrs. Parker, Lethbridge, and Gardiner go down to the Bull Ring on the night named. There were 250 to 300 people present and he took the names and addresses of the speakers and told them that they were acting contrary to the by-laws.

'The police did not interfere with the meeting, which dealt with the Labour question and public rights on the Hoe. It was an orderly meeting. Inspector Warne corroborated.

'Mr JH Trehane, acting for the accused, said that the defendants, either rightly or wrongly, had an impression that the Bull Ring was not part of the Hoe and did not come under the by-laws. They contended that any man had a right to go there at any time and speak on any subject he chose, or play a game; and he reminded the Bench that Sir Francis Drake was playing bowls there when the Armada was sighted. If their worships found against Mr Salter, he asked that the case might be stated for a superior court.

'The Town Clerk said that as it was a clear and simple matter of fact the court would not take it up.

'Their worships fined the defendant 20 shillings and 11 shillings costs and agreed to state a case on formal application being received from Mr Trehane within seven days.

'John T Parker, JW Gardner and Joseph Lethbridge were fined in like amounts and costs for a similar offence committed at the same time and place.' *(ibid)*

Top: *The Hoe with Smeaton's Tower, the Camera Obscura, and the Corporation Seat.*
Bottom: *The Camera has gone and the Colonnaded Belvedere erected in its place above the former Bull Ring.*

The Hoe in the snow - note the high fence around the Bull Ring.

Alderman King's Queen Victoria Jubilee Fountain was by no means the first fountain in the Hoe Park.

In November 1880 52-year-old Mrs Marianne Norrington wrote to the *Western Morning News* expressing the hope that a fountain might be placed on the Hoe in order that tired and thirsty children might be able to refresh themselves.

Mrs Norrington had been a regular visitor to the Hoe over the years, with different combinations of her ten children — six daughters and four sons — and had observed how hot boys and girls became in their play and how distressed they would get for want of water.

There were, too, the 'girls who had perhaps dragged up some heavy baby from Higher Street or Briton Street and had no means of satisfying their thirst.'

Sadly, Mrs Norrington passed away just a few months after her missive was published and her husband, 'being desirous of raising some memorial to one so much lamented,' thought he could do no better than carry out what was her own wish.

Consequently on a hot sunny day in June, this fine fountain was unveiled ... 'Presented to the town of Plymouth by Charles Norrington in memory of his wife Marianne Norrington 1881. Thirsty and ye gave me drink (a quote from St Matthew, 25:35).' *(Comet 1893)*

Mrs Norrington's husband, Charles was the son of a Bedford Street hosier and glover:

'In early life he became interested in agricultural chemistry and not only studied his subject in books, but took practical lessons on a farm belonging to his father at Lamerton near Tavistock. He lectured to the farmers, and soon became an authority upon the important subject of artificial manures.

'In 1846 he established the first artificial manure manufactory in the West of England and has been connected with this large and lucrative industry ever since. Commencing in a small way at the Commercial Wharf, he was able, in 1854, to start much more extensive works at Cattedown, since which time they have grown to very important dimensions, employing a great number of hands. The firm has a large foreign trade, besides an extensive home connection.

'In local business matters, Mr Norrington has always been foremost, and in social and philanthropic works he has never been lacking.

'In politics he is a conservative of the old school, and first entered the Council as a member for Vintry Ward as long ago as 1852.

'In 1863 he became Mayor of the Borough and did good service in that capacity. He was re-elected in 1864, and in the following year he had the honour of receiving the Prince and Princess of Wales, who visited Plymouth on the occasion of the Royal Agricultural Show being held in the town.

'Mr Norrington, as Mayor, also received General Garibaldi, in passing through Plymouth in April 1864.

'Behind the veil of domestic life Mr Norrington has suffered severely from pressure of the hand of death. Time has now happily smoothed the keen edges of sorrow or we should not refer to these events:

'In 1877, his eldest son, Charles Henry, died at the early age of 25; in 1881 he lost his second son, Harold, and in the same year, he was bereft of his much respected wife, in memory of whom he erected the fountain.

'In memory of his sons, he presented the Carillon and Westminster chimes to St Andrew's Church, and a new aisle to St John's, Sutton on Plym.' *(ibid)*

Norrington's Fountain, sculpted by Samuel Trevenen. The 20-foot-high memorial is modelled on Rebecca of the Well. Inset: Charles Norrington.

1879: Work begins on the construction of the fourth light on the Eddystone Reef — the foundation stone was a 3½-ton block of Wadebridge granitie, landed in June 1879.

A week or two before Norrington's Fountain was unveiled on the Hoe, 14 miles out to sea, on 1 June 1881, the Duke of Edinburgh stepped off HMS *Lively* when passing up the English Channel, and laid the final stone in the construction of James Douglass's Eddystone lighthouse.

The foundation stone was laid by the Duke (who was then Master of Trinity House) a little under two years earlier, in August 1879. It wasn't until 18 May 1882, however, that the new lantern was ready to be lit. Once again the Duke of Edinburgh officiated and a few weeks later James Douglass received a letter from the Prime Minister, William Gladstone, telling him that the Queen proposed to confer upon him a knighthood.

The son of Nicholas Douglass, one of the principal lighthouse engineers of his day and brother of William Douglass, Engineer in Chief to the Irish Lighthouse Authority, James Douglass truly had lighthouse construction in his blood. It was no great surprise when James was, in turn, appointed Engineer-in-Chief to Trinity House in 1862. Neither did it alarm anyone that, engaged upon other engineering concerns for Trinity House, he left much of the work on the Eddystone project to his son, William Tregerthen Douglass. After the final stone had been laid William spent much of that first winter, before the new light was lit, observing Smeaton's tower.

'The waves, striking the old tower at its foundation, ran up the surface with great force, unimpeded by any projection until arriving at the lantern gallery, where they were partially broken up by the cornice, and then expended themselves in heavy spray over the lantern, entirely excluding from view, for the space of half a minute, any portion of the tower or lantern. By contrast at the new tower, the heavy seas striking the cylindrical base were immediately broken up, and rushed around the opposite side, the sprays only ascending to the height of the lantern gallery.'

Below left: *Plan of Smeaton's lighthouse, showing the method of dovetailing the stonework.* Below middle: *A cross-section of Smeaton's Tower detailing the accommodation available.* Below: *Douglass's finished structure alongside the stump of the Smeaton structure. Douglass's lighthouse was twice as tall and four times as large as Smeaton's, it had nine rooms as opposed to four and it contained 2,171 blocks of granite weighing 4,688 tons.*

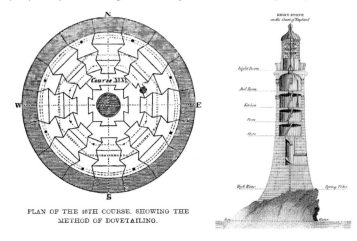

PLAN OF THE 16TH COURSE, SHOWING THE METHOD OF DOVETAILING.

Smeaton's Tower: Reconstructed on Plymouth Hoe between October 1882 and September 1884.
Inset: *The bronze halfpenny from 1860 with a representation of Smeaton's Tower behind Britannia.*
Inset left: *John Pethick*

The rationale behind the need for a new light on the reef had been a concern for some years.

The main worry was that the rock supporting Smeaton's structure had been undermined and was no longer safe and the volume of shipping using the Channel meant that Trinity House could not afford the prospect of not being able to provide a warning.

In 1877 the British Association held its annual assembly here in Plymouth. James Douglass was one of the speakers and in his presentation he described how the undermining had become worse. Furthermore, much of the cement on the Smeaton light had decayed and that they were proposing to replace Smeaton's tower with a new one, one that Douglass was already working on.

Smeaton's light had already, by this stage, become a national treasure. In 1860, shortly after Smeaton's light celebrated its centenary, a representation of the iconic structure had been created on the reverse of the British penny and halfpenny (and it remained there for many years). Not surprisingly, therefore, Douglass's news provoked a national outcry.

Parliament considered the issue. There was a suggestion that if the reef was not safe, why not remove it? To which the answer came that the cost of blowing up some two million tons of rock would be at least seven times the cost of building a new tower.

And so a new tower was built. But what was to happen to Smeaton's tower? Why not, suggested Frederick Webb, a schoolmaster who was running an academic institution in Portland Villas, rebuild the original lighthouse on the Hoe, on the site of the Trinity obelisk?

A subscription was raised and John Pethick, who had recently erected the first hotel to appear on the Hoe — the Grand — agreed to provide a new base for the iconic structure. On 20 October 1882 the Duke of Edinburgh was on hand once more to lay the foundation stone for the rebuilding. On 24 September 1884 the work was completed.

'Today marked the consummation of the work. The Deputy Master of Trinity House (Captain Webb) and the Elder Brethren attended. A Corporation procession, consisting of the Mayor of Plymouth, and a number of Mayors of Devon and Cornwall, was formed at the Plymouth Guildhall. These met the Trinity Brethren at the Lighthouse, where there was a great gathering of spectators. On the arrival of the procession the National Anthem was played by a band of Gordon Highlanders, and a dedication prayer was offered up by the Rev. Prebendary Wilkinson, vicar of Plymouth. Mr CF Burnard, as Chairman of the Executive Committee, in whose hands was the custody of the tower, then formally asked the Deputy Master of Trinity House to accept an ornamental key.

'Captain Webb, having suitably acknowledged the receipt of the Tower as symbolised by the key, then presented the key to the Mayor (Mr John Greenway) who unlocked the Lighthouse and formally took over the custody of the structure on behalf of the Corporation and the Town.

'The Mayor then thanked the Deputy Master of the Trinity Corporation for their generous aid in carrying out the work, and the proceedings shortly afterwards concluded with votes of thanks.

'In the evening a banquet in honour of the occasion was held in St Andrew's Hall under the presidency of the Mayor. It was also attended by Captain Webb, the Deputy Master, Captains Burns, Fenwick, Vivian, and Weare, the Earl of Morley, Under Secretary of State for War, Mr P Stewart Maciver MP, and Admiral Sir Houston Stewart, Naval Commander-in-Chief.

'Subsequent to the dinner a reception was held by the Mayor in the Plymouth Guildhall, at which about 800 guests were present. The building was magnificently decorated for the occasion.' (TSG 1884)

An advertisement for the position of caretaker of the Tower attracted 78 applicants. The wage was set at 15 shillings a week.

Top: *Jubilee bonfire*. Bottom: *General shot of Plymouth Hoe decked out in readiness for the Queen's Jubilee in 1897.*

Mr Boehm's noble work stands on a pedestal of polished red Aberdeen granite, weighing nine tons, which in its turn rests upon a base of Cornish granite laid on top of three slabs from the Penryn quarries. The designs were prepared by Messrs. Hine & Odgers, architects, of Lockyer Street. Inset: William Derry Mayor 1861-63 1879-80

A little earlier in Mayor Greenway's Mayoralty, another major event took place on Plymouth Hoe — the unveiling of the statue of Sir Francis Drake. 'It would be difficult, perhaps, to say with any pretence to accuracy when the suggestion to commemorate the name and fame of Sir Francis Drake by a statue, or some other monument on Plymouth Hoe was first made. Nearly everybody who has written about the Hoe has had something to say about it. But it is to the Rev WS Lach-Syzrma that the credit belongs of having been the first to make a practical proposal; in fact he deserves to be remembered as the chief originator of the movement.'

Mr Lach-Syzrma's suggestion, made in October 1880, in a letter to the *Western Daily Mercury*, was in favour of a memorial to celebrate the tercentenary of Drake's return from his voyage of circumnavigation. The idea was warmly approved and advocated by the *Western Daily Mercury*, and it was afterwards taken up by Mr William Derry, the Mayor of Plymouth, who, at a Volunteer prize distribution meeting, offered a first subscription towards the fund of £50. Mr FA Morrish, his successor in the Mayoralty, entered into the undertaking with a sympathetic spirit.

'The matter was brought before a meeting of the Town Council by Mr James Moon and on November 26, in the Guildhall, the following resolution was unanimously adopted: "That this meeting is of the opinion that the eminent services rendered to the nation by Sir Francis Drake, foremost of England's navigators, and one of her most prominent naval commanders, call for recognition, and should be commemorated by a memorial."

'A resolution was submitted in favour of a statue or group of statues, an idea which Mr Lancaster had originated in a paper read before the Plymouth Debating Society.

'In spite of the cordial help rendered by the Press at home, on the continent, and in our colonies — in spite also of the Mansion House meeting and patronage of the Prince of Wales and many influential noblemen — the thing seemed to hang fire, the subscription list remained at a low figure, and at Midsummer, 1882, the treasurer had only a few hundred pounds in hand.

'In the course of the year the people of Tavistock bestirred with the object of getting a Drake Memorial for their own town; and on appealing to the Duke of Bedford for help, he with characteristic generosity, offered to defray the whole cost of a statue and present it to the people of Tavistock.

'His Grace commissioned Mr Boehm to execute a statue in bronze, at a cost of about £4,000; and the Plymouth committee, finding it impossible to carry out their original design, obtained his Grace's permission to produce a replica of it.' (DC 1884)

Top: Looking north with Norrington's Fountain to the left. Bottom: Looking east. Edgar Boehm was born in Vienna in 1834 and settled in Britain in 1862. From 1865 onwards he enjoyed a virtual monopoly in providing statues of public figures and royalty, including Queen Victoria, Darwin (for the Natural History Museum), Carlyle and William Tyndale (on the Embankment) and Wellington (on Hyde Park Corner)

'The ceremony of unveiling the Drake Statue was performed at noon, on Thursday (14 February 1884), by Lady Elliot Drake, of Nutwell Court, near Exeter. A capital programme had been arranged for the occasion and, favoured by fine weather, all the details were carried out with scarcely a hitch from beginning to end.

'So gloomy was the prospect on Wednesday afternoon that a member of the Town Council felt impelled to express his anxiety for the fate of the three thousand school children who were to be marshalled on the Hoe without shelter.

'The day's programme comprised military, naval, and volunteer displays, and processions of corporate and other public bodies and school children, a luncheon in the Guildhall after the ceremony on the Hoe, and a concert and exhibition of Drake relics.

'The day was observed in the Three Towns as a general holiday and it will not be far wide of the mark if we say that while the ceremony of unveiling was in progress there could not have been many short of 18,000 or 20,000 present. (ibid)

William Wright, together with composer John Hele wrote a Grand Choral March, 'Sir Francis Drake', that was performed that day with a chorus of 1,000 children joining the Company of the Theatre Royal. 'The tradesmen of the town, responded well to the appeal to decorate their premises in honour of the event. Bedford Street, Westwell Street, and George Street were profusely decorated with banners. There was also a good display in Lockyer Street and the vicinity of the Hoe. In Old Town Street, Mr Rowse, ironmonger, exhibited a large picture of the bombardment of Alexandria, and an inscription which asked for "All honour to our British sailors, the descendants of Sir Francis Drake."

'It may be mentioned here that the proposal to establish a Drake Memorial Museum has been carried into effect in connection with the Athenaeum. The museum was opened sometime last year, under the presidency of Mr RN Worth, and it is accessible to the general public at stated times.'(DC 1884)

'The origin of the Armada Memorial may be traced back to the unveiling of the fine cast of Sir Francis Drake. Mr Wright, the Borough Librarian at Plymouth, and others associated with him on that occasion, felt that something ought to be done to commemorate in a more complete manner the deeds, not only of Sir Francis Drake, but all of the Armada heroes. As, however, Her Majesty's Jubilee then filled the minds of the public, nothing was attempted until the end of the summer of 1887, when a small meeting was held at Mr Wright's residence, and a scheme formulated.

'The first idea was to make the Drake statue the nucleus of a larger group, in which the other chief actors concerned should figure, but other views prevailed. A committee was formed with Wright as secretary and numerous suggestions were made as to what form the memorial should take. Among them, and including the addition to the Drake statue, were the formation of a "Drake Institute" for old and decayed sailor of the merchant service, an historical pageant, an exhibition of Elizabethan pictures, a marine display in the Sound, bonfires and beacon lights, and even an insurance company for insuring fishermen's lives and property.

'None, however, met with unanimous approval, and it was at last suggested by the Rev W Bians that the erection of a memorial column or tower — inscribed not only with the names of Drake and Raleigh, but of the other heroes who contributed to the defeat of the Armada — would be a suitable manner in which to commemorate the great event.' (D&EDG 1890)

In April 1888, Mayor Henry Waring wrote an open letter from the Drake Chamber of the Guildhall requesting official support for the project. 'Since the matter was first mooted a considerable amount of attention has been brought to bear upon the subject, public opinion has been aroused, the press, both London and Provincial, has expressed approval of the scheme, and a large and steadily increasing section has declared in favour of celebrating, in some appropriate manner the tercentenary of so great a crisis in our national history. Into the details of the history of that time it is needless to enter; it is sufficient to say that the significance of the event cannot be over estimated, for to the providential deliverance of this country from Spanish invasion and foreign sway, the English speaking race the world over, is largely indebted for liberty and privileges it now enjoys.

'At public meetings held in the Guildhall, Plymouth, in November and December last Resolutions favourable to the project were almost unanimously adopted and a large and influential committee — with the Mayor of Plymouth as Chairman — was appointed to consider in what way those Resolutions could best be carried into effect.

'In response to advertisements inserted in various representative journals, the committee obtained designs for the proposed memorial. From amongst a large number of suitable and well executed drawings, the design of Mr Herbert A Gribble, ARIBA, of South Kensington (the talented architect of Brompton Oratory), was selected.

Opposite page: *Hoe Promenade with Drake's Statue, bandstand and Armada Memorial - also above in 1891.*

'The design consists of a granite pedestal, surmounted by a figure of Britannia, with the shield of the three crosses, a banner and trident in her left hand, and in her right, a sword.

'Below there are twelve wreaths of laurel, and in the panels of the shaft, medallion portraits of Haward, Drake, Hawkins, Raleigh, Seymour, Wintour, Frobisher and others, with their respective coats of arms.

'... Although Plymouth and its neighbourhood were more closely connected with the actual event than towns in the northern or midland counties, yet, as all were equally interested in the defeat of the invasion, we feel that the movement should obtain general support, and we therefore solicit co-operation.' (Waring 1888)

The National Armada Memorial was unveiled by the Duke of Edinburgh, then Naval Commander-in-Chief at Devonport, on Tuesday, 21 October 1890. It was erected by national subscription.

This page and opposite top: *1877 Construction work begins on the new Plymouth Marine Laboratory.* Bottom: *1888, the finished article.*

The Armada Memorial was by no means the only development on the Hoe to receive national attention and indeed national funding.

On 1 November 1884 the Secretary of the Royal Society wrote to Professor E Ray Lankester, Secretary of the Marine Biological Society: 'Sir, Your letter relative to the Marine Biological Association was laid before the council at their meeting on Thursday last and I am directed to inform you that the council have voted the sum of £250 from the "donation fund" in aid of the Marine Biological Association, as a token of their sympathy with an effort which they have every reason to believe will contribute largely to the progress of biological science in this country.' *(LES 1884)*

The Association was incorporated (earlier in 1884) 'under the Act relating to associations not aiming at commercial profits.

'Its primary object [as of June 1884] is to establish a thoroughly well organised laboratory on the English coast, where the study of marine zoology, and botany may be carried on by naturalists — as at Naples, at Roscoff, in France and at Beaufort and other institutions in the United States. These studies will be especially directed to such questions as oyster breeding, and the spawning, food, and habits of sea fish, so as to provide knowledge which is urgently needed by our various fishery industries. His Royal Highness the Prince of Wales has become patron of the association, and has, besides expressing his great interest in the success of the enterprise which the association has in hand, contributed a handsome donation to the building fund. Ten thousand pounds are needed to establish the laboratory. Those who desire to aid scientific men in this really national enterprise should communicate with the secretary of the association, Professor Ray Lankester, of University College, London.

'The claims of Plymouth, Weymouth, and of Bangor, in North Wales, as the most suitable sites for the laboratory, are now under the consideration of the council of the association. The natural advantages of these three localities are so nearly balanced that a donation of a few thousand pounds from anyone interested in one of them would determine the location of the laboratory on the site favoured by the donor.' *(BA July 1884)*

The donation from the Royal Society turned out to be one of many: 'At a meeting of the council of the Association on Wednesday 5 November, in the rooms of the Linnean Society, votes of thanks were passed to the Clothworkers' Company for a donation of £500, to

the Mercers' Company for one of 250 guineas, and to the British Association for one of £150. The total sum as yet subscribed in the aid of the objects of the Association was announced by the treasurer Mr Crisp, as amounting to between £4,000 and £5,000, with 109 annual subscribers.

'On the report of the committee appointed to examine the Plymouth site for the erection of the proposed marine laboratory, consisting of Prof Ray Lankester, Mr Charles Stewart, and Mr Spencer Bate, all of whom were present, it was resolved that this site on the Citadel hill should be adopted.' *(EEN 8 Nov 1894)*

The decision to set up in Plymouth was helped in no small measure by the offer received from the Town Council with regard to both a site and financial assistance from local benefactors, among them John and Robert Bayly, who had agreed substantial financial support after being canvassed by C Spence Bate, the celebrated expert on crustacea.

Locally it doubtless helped that the Council, in turn, had only recently (in 1885) been offered a lease on the glacis and trenches to the south of the Citadel.

Thus it was that the £13,000 Plymouth Marine Laboratory was successfully opened on Saturday 30 June 1888.

'The opening ceremony was performed by Professor Flower who explained that the recent Fisheries Exhibition had aroused the country to the importance of developing the food supply of which our seas were capable, and this had led to the establishment of the Plymouth Laboratory, the Government having liberally granted the site for the institution on Citadel Hill, and having made also a grant of £500 a year for five years towards its maintenance.

'The scheme had received support from the Prince of Wales and the Fishmongers' Company, the latter being a munificent patron.

'The station starts with an income of £900 a year. The staff will consist of a resident director, Mr Gilbert Bourne, and two naturalists, Mr JD Cunningham, of Oxford, and Mr WTR Weldon, of St John's College, Cambridge, a young naturalist who has already shown capacity for original research. There will also be attached an engineer and his wife, a fisherman, and two boys, to which modest staff, as funds increase, necessary additions will be made.

'Moreover students will be received, who will pay fees for instruction. The Fishmongers' Company of London have made a donation of £2,000 to the funds.

'At the banquet given by the Worshipful Company of Fishmongers in connection with the opening ceremony, Earl Morley remarked that it was strange that a people so favoured as our own had lagged so long in the rear of other countries in the scientific investigation of the harvest of the sea.

'Professor Ray Lankester, replying on behalf of the Association, said the dream of his life had been realized in this event, and that the greatest good must result, since it was impossible for investigation honestly conducted to be purposeless in its results.' (WT 2 July 1888)

Top: *The new building sits serenely on the slopes of Citadel Hill.* Bottom: *30 June 1888, opening of the Plymouth Marine Laboratory. Among the dignitaries: The Mayors of Plymouth and Devonport, the Vicar of St Andrew's Archdeacon Wilkinson, historian RN Worth, Prof E Ray Lankester (one of the prime movers) and E Spence Bate. Inset: Architect Henry Snell.*

The new building was designed principally by local architect Henry Snell, who worked in conjunction with the Council of the Association and the War Department, from whom the site was being leased (the site had then, until very recently, been within the confines of the outer works of the Royal Citadel).

No sooner had work been completed on the new Marine building than there was a proposal to construct a carriage roadway around the front of the Citadel. The outworks of the fortification were levelled and the Town negotiated a 99-year lease for the land that had now become available. As well as the new road the works were to consist of a bridge across the Submarine Mining Establishment around from Fisher's Nose which was to be continued by a tunnel.

The Colonel commanding the Royal Engineers was prepared to allow the route, but not any attendant rights of way being granted. The Corporation were expected to pick up the bill for all this work, but it was to be understood that the bridge, which was to be roofed in order to prevent anything — stones or whatever — being dropped from the sides, was to be the property of the War Office.

A mixture of steam and sail in the Sound. Elder & Company, one of the many operators working out of the port, ran the sailing clipper Torrens from here to Adelaide until 1891.

Pre-dating many of these recent developments on the Hoe was the erection of the Lookout House on the Hoe promontory.

'This is for the shelter of the officers of shipping agents and others, on the look out for mail steamers, many of which call at this port to land mails and passengers.'

Plymouth had already been serving as a mailship port of call for some 20 years by this point. It was in December 1850 *The Plymouth and Devonport Weekly Journal* had announced that: 'It now affords us very great satisfaction to be able to state that it has definitely been arranged that the mails for the Cape of Good Hope shall be despatched from the Port of Plymouth. The vessels to be used on this service are screw steamers, of considerable power. The first of these, the *Bosphorus*, under Captain JV Hall, will leave Plymouth on the noon of the 15th inst. and one of the company's steamers will also leave this port on the 15th of every succeeding month for the Cape, calling at Madeira and Sierra Leone.'

As it transpired the *Bosphorus* left a day late. A grand procession of Magistrates, Aldermen, Councillors and the Mayors of Plymouth and Devonport, as well as postal officials, sailors and military bands escorted the mails from the Post Office at the top of St Andrew Street to Millbay Pier where seven bags were loaded on to the General Screw Steam Shipping Company vessel. The auspicious day was a wet and windy one. Nevertheless, it was the commencement of 'a new commercial era and we do not doubt that the port will be found in all respects efficient for the service.' (*P&DWJ 5 December 1850*)

As this trade expanded so too did the importance increase of being able to alert waiting tenders and trains to the imminent arrival of mailships. Hence the construction of the Lookout so that this job could be done in comparative comfort in the event of inclement weather.

The Mail ships were served, from the 1870s onwards, by specially commissioned tenders, the *Sir Francis Drake* (from 1873) and *Sir Walter Raleigh* (from 1876).

The mailships, however, didn't mark the beginning of the Port's ocean passenger trade, that had already been for a decade or so as emigration vessels took convicts and those looking to start a new life to the Cape, Australia and New Zealand — the Colonial Land and Emigration Commissioners offered assisted passages — free even, if you were a married couple, under 35 and heading for Australia.

Top: *Crowds enjoying the sunshine around the Lookout.* Bottom: *Uniformed mailship men on the look out.*

Over the course of the Nineteenth Century swimming has become increasingly popular. From the earliest times the activity was regulated, although perhaps not always successfully.

There had been bathing at Pebble Side before the Queen came to the throne, but it wasn't until 1843 that the first man-made steps to the sea were formed. Four years later there was an application to erect bathing-huts and a three-bay, vaulted-brick structure was built overlooking Reform Beach.

A urinal was installed in 1851 and the western areas of the Hoe became increasingly male dominated. Bathing costumes were uncommon prior to this time and the majority of men swam naked.

In 1860 there was an increase in the number of public bathing-places and a flight of steps was made on the eastern side of the main bathing beach, for the benefit of the fairer sex, with a screen wall erected to form an eastern boundary. A ladies' bathing-pool was created around the natural rock pools that existed, between the Shag Pool and Tin Side. A separate facility for men was created towards the eastern end of the Hoe. Meanwhile, the construction of the Pier created further demand for swimming facilities. It was decided to concrete part of the natural basin and an additional storey of dressing-house was put up, capable of accommodating 88 bathers.

In the summer of 1885 'A report was received from the Hoe and Recreation Ground Committee recommending the acceptance of tenders for the construction of an open corrugated-iron shed at the ladies' bathing place and for the erection of additions to the ladies' dressing-house at the ladies' bathing place.' (WMN 18 June 1885)

The area was for ladies exclusively from 6am to 9.30pm between the 1 May and 1 October. The wearing of dresses or bathing-drawers was to be compulsory for all bathers except those under twelve years old. Mrs Grant, the woman in charge of the Ladies' Bathing Place from 6am to 5pm each day, was awarded a pay rise from 5/3d a week to 14/- a week — a substantial increase.

There were improvements too to the men's facilities with seats cut into the rock face. There were further complaints from the boatmen, however, that men were bathing naked after 9am and in 1893 it was decided to detail an extra constable on the Hoe to monitor the situation. The previous year, incidentally, improvement works included the depositing of 200 loads of sand at Tinside and a number of rocks were smoothed and broken for the benefit of bathers.

An attempt to make a more significant improvement came in 1897, however, when Mr Giovanni Trafani was tasked with preparing a model for a new bathing scheme as devised by the Borough Surveyor.

Top left: *bathers off Pebble Beach*. Top right: *Swimmers on the Pier*.

In the 1850s it was estimated that 400 to 500 females bathed daily under the Hoe and a similar number of men.

The second half of the Nineteenth Century witnessed a great many improvements to the swimming facilities on the Hoe waterfront. However, far more people paddle than swim and there have been many fatalities from young people getting themselves into difficulties in local creeks, rivers and the sea.

Top left: *Ladies at the seaside.*
Top right: *Bathing beneath the Pier.*
Left: *Crowds enjoying the sun on the Hoe.*
Below: *Some new bathing facilities.*

While the Hoe waterfront and the Hoe Park have been allowed to retain much of their natural form over the reign of Queen Victoria, there is a very different story to be told at West Hoe. At the beginning of the Twentieth Century here, too, were grassy expanses gradually sloping down to the water's edge at Rusty Anchor and Millbay.

In 1818 Thomas Gill started an alkali and soap factory on the north-east banks of Millbay. It was an ideal location, lime and brine being basic components of the burgeoning chemical industries. Gill built small quays to serve his quarry, which he later linked up with a small dock in the quarry itself, by means of a canal that passed under a footbridge of what was to become Radford Road. This came out into Millbay a little over 100 yards to the north of Millbay Pier that Gill had been empowered to construct in 1840. Mr Gill also built a row of cottages at the top of the Hoe for the quarry men he employed. But not everyone was taken with his endeavours:

Rusty Anchor and Drake's Island, late-1840s.

'In the 'Forties and 'Fifties an army of navies were at work with such effect, that in the course of a few years, quite half of your Hoe (of Drake's Hoe! Think of it! — if he had been living then, I am quite sure it would never have happened), well, quite half of your Hoe was quarried away for the sake of the stone it yielded! Just fancy such a thing — my blood boils — oh the soft backbones of the authorities — nay, they had no backbones, they were invertebrates and should have been born jellyfish. But it is of no use losing my temper — the thing is done.' (SW)

Done it was and West Hoe was flattened, thereby rendering it eminently suitable for residential development. Ambitious plans were revealed for a proposed West Hoe Town and on Thursday 6 June 1850 the first stone was laid in a block of nine properties that were to become West Hoe Terrace.

Meanwhile, as this development was going ahead Thomas Gill, who had served the town as Mayor in 1836 and represented Plymouth in Parliament between 1841-47 as a Liberal MP, agreed, as the owner of the West Hoe Estate, to lease land at Two Coves to allow the construction of indoor public baths.

Previously Plymouth had enjoyed such facilities in Union Street, on the edge of the street named in their honour — Bath Street. These had been opened on 1 May 1830 by Sir Byam Martin 'acting as proxy for his present Majesty.' However after barely 20 years the Royal Union Baths, as they had been styled, were demolished as they lay on the line of the proposed railway into Millbay.

There followed a wilderness period with no indoor 'proprietary bathing' available in the area. Various plans were drawn up, but little happened for five or six years until, in September 1857, it was decided that any proposals for free bathing should be independent of plans for 'proprietary bathing'. To that end the Local Board of Health and the Corporation each put £200 towards improving the free-bathing facilities — mentioned above — and on 15 July 1858, Mayor Richard Hicks laid the foundation stone for the new West Hoe Baths at Two Coves Quay.

Designed by Messrs Damant & Reed, the new facility included showers, vapour plunge, douche as well as hot and cold baths for both sexes. A 'large and elegant' promenade saloon and reading room occupied the front of the building and afforded panoramic views of the Sound.

A 25-foot-wide carriage drive dropped down from the main road to the entrance and the whole structure was designed so as not to impede the view from that road. A sea wall ran around the perimeter of the site and was regarded as 'an important feature.' Constructed of local limestone it was surrounded by an ornamental balustrade.

The completed West Hoe Terrace — note the land flattened by Gill's quarrying in the foreground.

These two developments, however, were but a small part of a much more grandiose scheme.

The intention was that West Hoe was to become a credit to the West of England with fine new streets, villas, hotels, a church and even a vast aquarium nestled under the Hoe Cliff on the site of West Hoe Park. Alfred Norman and Alfred Gribble were the architects who drew up the blueprint and Gribble's drawing made it look very impressive indeed.

Progress was slow though. T Duncan Newton had become West Hoe's first new resident in the middle house of the Terrace a year or so later and the four houses on either side soon followed but, for the next 30 years or so, the terrace stood in splendid isolation. Pier Street, Grand Parade and Radford Street proper, were not completed until after the Hoe Pier had been erected

The long drawn-out process of developing West Hoe meant that for many years there were two large vacant plots just above the baths. These have proved an ideal location on which to site visiting fairs and circuses, of which, notably from the 1890s onwards, there has been an increasing number. Doubtless the construction of the Pavilion Pier and the West Hoe Pier, made this a veritable honeypot for tourists and holidaymakers.

Top: West Hoe Terrace in splendid isolation - note the Millbay Custom House (inspiration for the Hoe Lookout Tower?) on the right. Middle: West Hoe development under way. Note the 1880s harbour created infront of the late 1850s West Hoe Baths. Bottom: Alfred Norman and Herbert Gribble's plans for the West Hoe Town proposals. Right: Sanger's Circus comes to the Hoe.

Top and Bottom: *Hancock's travelling showground comes to West Hoe around the turn of the century. The intoxicating proximity of the Pavilion Pier, the tram-stops and the steamer drop-on and hop-off point, providing a huge draw to young and old.*

47

By the 1890s the Hoe Park had consolidated its status as a very fine attraction with additions and developments in the previous decade or so making a considerable impact — many of them visible in whole, or in part, from this vantage point (upstairs in the Grand Hotel): from left to right, the Armada Memorial (1888), Drake's Statue (1884), Marine Biological Association (1888), Smeaton's Tower (1884), the Colonnaded Belvedere (1891) and the Pavilion Pier (1891). In 1890, the Hoe Promenade, being found to be in a very unsatisfactory condition after wet weather, was 'tar paved with stone from West Hoe'. Cornelius Laskey Duke, road contractor, was awarded the contract for a quote of £1,158.

By the beginning of the 1890s the Hoe had been quite transformed, but not necessarily to everyone's satisfaction:

'The improvements have been most thorough, but they have had the effect of banishing the youth of the town from what, from time immemorial, had been their playground.

'Time was when the Hoe Park, that is the portion nearest the town, was given up almost entirely to our young men and lads for cricket and football, and woe betide the hapless pedestrian who ventured within the radius of the wickets.

'The authorities were wise to forbid these games to be played in a place of such general resort, but they have not provided our youths with other recreation grounds. For a while they were permitted to use Freedom Field, but since that place has been turned into a Park and planted with flowers and shrubs, our boys have been compelled to seek fresh vantage ground.

'True, a field near Mount Gould has been set apart for recreative purposes, but this is not enough, and the Corporation should speedily provide other and more suitable places for the exercise of the National Games, which, while to some extent dangerous, are yet conducive to the health and physical development of the rising generation. It is undesirable that footballing should be carried on in the streets and public squares, but youth must have its sports, and it is the duty of the Corporation to provide the wherewithal.

'Beaumont Park, beautiful and convenient though it be for a quiet saunter or restful lounge, is yet unsuited for the games in which our boys delight; and we hope the day is not far distant when the great desideratum of a Recreation Ground for all classes and conditions will be supplied on that large waste piece of ground bordered by the Three Towns at Deadlake. It should be a recreation ground pure and simple, not a park.' *(Wright 1894)*

Right: *Simple pleasures on the Hoe.* Left: *Victoria Park, in practical use for recreation from the mid 1890s, officially opened in 1902.*

49

'At the east end of the Hoe is the Citadel, covering the entrances to the Cattewater and Sutton Pool. The entrance to the Citadel is on the north side; it admits to an esplanade which is adorned with a statue of George II in the guise of a Roman warrior. On the south side there is a fort for the protection of the Sound. It is advisable in visiting this important fortress to take a walk along the ramparts, some three-quarters of a mile in extent, and see the fine and varied views, with their foreground embrassures, solid wall and formidable artillery.

'Up until 1860 Plymouth possessed no more important fortification, but in that year a Royal Commission recommended the building of a chain of forts to encircle the 'Three Towns' from Tregantle on the west to Staddon on the east, and that has been done. These are land defences; the sea defences consist of the Breakwater Fort, Picklecombe, Bovisand, Drake's Island and Garden Battery.

'The general armament of Plymouth is very suggestive of England's might, and it may be studied in detail by permission of the Officer in Command of the Engineers on the spot; it is wonderful how few persons are curious enough to avail themselves of the privilege.

'If strangers to Plymouth would first of all take a stroll around the ramparts they would obtain a clear view of the town generally, and of its harbours, the Cattewater and Hamoaze.' (DH&P c1897)

As can be seen from a comparison of the two images accompanying this text, up until 1888 there was bridge leading into the Citadel — it was one of two: 'After passing the palisadoes the visitor will cross the counter-scarp by a drawbridge, and then pass through a gateway bearing the Royal Arms, and fitted with portcullis and gates, and protected by cannon. He will then cross the ditch by a wooden bridge to the inner gate [shown here], which bears on the entablature, the date 1670. (Wright 1879)

The removal of the outer gate, the ditch and bridge were all part of a major review following a report commissioned in 1885 by Major-General Porter, CRE Western District.

The outer defences of the Citadel by this time were of little practical value and there was pressure from the people of Plymouth to release the land so it could be added to, or rather returned to the Hoe; and in 1888 that is precisely what happened. The whole of the lower fort was demolished and Hoe walks were extended for the first time as far around the front as Fisher's Nose 'thus affording to the inhabitants and visitors the most delightful and diversified panorama of the surroundings.'

Left: *The bridge (seen on the opposite page) is gone.*
Top: *The entrance to the new walkway that was constructed to allow pedestrians passage from the Hoe to the Barbican.*
Bottom: *The Barbican entrance to the link.*

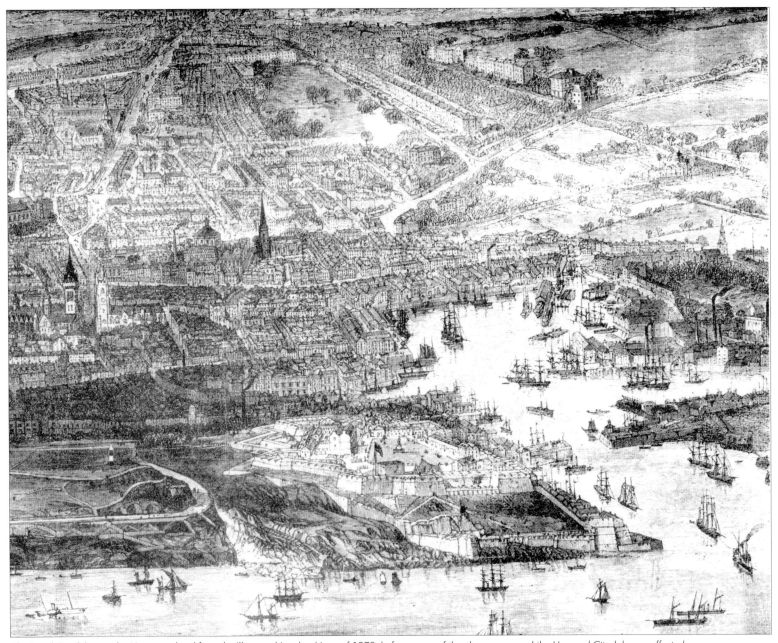

The Royal Citadel upon the Hoe — a detail from the Illustrated London News of 1873, before many of the changes around the Hoe and Citadel were effected.

Another gate that was deemed expendable around the same time was the historic Hoe Gate. This was the last of the town gates to be demolished — Friary, Gasking, Frankfurt, Martyn's, Old Town, Coxside and South Gate were all 'removed' at various times between 1763 and 1863. Demolition of the gate, however, was not brought about entirely by 'a spirit of utilitarianism'; for although it did, to some extent, get in the way of the Corporation's plans for widening the streets in the area, 'decency' was also said 'to forbid its continued existence'. It had, apparently, become a favourite haunt for courting couples.

So it was that in 1863 Thomas Were Fox, the owner of the gate, after reserving some of the architectural ornaments and 'the crook of guineas buried in the basement' for himself, sold off the gate for £44.

There is, incidentally, a suggestion that as some of the details of the lower stonework are similar to the Sally port, and other gates of the Citadel, Hoe Gate may well have been carved by the same mason.

The Hoe Gate is removed.

The Hoe Gate at the top of Hoe Gate Street.

THE STREETS OF OLD PLYMOUTH

At the dawn of the Nineteenth Century there were two gateways into that Elizabethan suburb centred around Southside Street — the Hoe Gate, as previously mentioned, demolished in 1863, and the South Gate or Barbican Gate, erected, according to our learned historian Llewellyn Jewitt, in 1602. '

'It stood at the Barbican just by the old Fort.'

Some 50 years later, the then lessee, Richard Vinson, 'built it over and by the side' of this Barbican or fortress by the water. Years later, sometime between 1790 and 1800, courtesy of our MP, Admiral John MacBride, the West Pier was built out in an easterly direction to extend almost as far as the East Pier, running in the opposite direction. In this way Sutton Harbour became even more of a safe haven than before.

The South Gate, or Barbican House as it was now styled, gradually became something of an inconvenience and in April 1830 we read that: 'Workmen are now employed in taking down that nuisance called Barbican House.'

The report added: 'We understand the Corporation has generously given the site on which it stands for the use of the public.' (NDJ 15 April 1830)

Some 30 years or so later the demolition men were back in the area to take down the two quaint and ancient properties to the south of the Island House.

This page and opposite: *Views of the Barbican showing the three-storey, dormer roofed houses demolished in the 1860s.*

'The Barbican itself generally presents a busy scene, for it is really the fish market of the district; and as we pass along we are sure to jostle against fishbuyers, fishermen, fishsellers, besides seamen of various nationalities; and if we mingle with the throng, we shall be almost deafened by the Babel of voices which greets our ears.

'A saunter on the Barbican in the early morning, soon after the arrival of the fishing fleet, is an interesting study for anyone who delights in noting the various phases of human nature.

'Sutton Pool, alongside which we are passing, is the anchorage ground of the fishing craft, which in good seasons congregate here from all parts of the coast, and, in general the market is a good one.' *(Wright 1879)*

Writing for the *Graphic Magazine* that same year, RN Worth waxed lyrical in a similar vein: 'There is no more picturesque or characteristic scene in Plymouth than that which the Barbican presents when the fishing boats, crowding all sail for early arrival, come in.

'In the height of the season the pool hard by is crowded with fishing boats, their brown sails flapping lazily in the puffs of breeze, which has brought them in.

Above: *Two views of the busy Barbican — note how close the ships are tied up to the houses opposite.*

A similar view looking south towards the old Watch House.

The Barbican (originally Southside Quay) with the Watch House more clearly visible. Within a few years of this image being taken the quay wall would be considerably extended towards the pool.

More early action on the Barbican.

'The Quay is filled with hundreds of maunds of fish, and lined with scores of carts.

'Hake, mackerel, turbots, whiting, plaice, flounder, pollack, mullet, John Dory, are among the fish most plentifully caught.

'Among the maunds and carts there is an eager and excited crowd — fishermen and fisherwomen, in costumes from which all distinctive character has not yet departed fish salesmen and fish buyers; and as the auction is held, and the pencil of the auctioneer falls upon his book, maund after maund is loaded into waiting carts, and off they go, full gallop through the narrow streets of the old town to the railway station.

'In half an hour the once busy scene is deserted: the Barbican is quiet again, and nothing is left behind but that "ancient and fishlike smell" which is the peculiar prerogative of such localities.' (*Worth 1878*)

Noisy as Worth and Wright might have found it at the end of the 1870s, by the end of the 1880s the din became louder still. In 1890, over 5,000 tons of fish were sent out of Plymouth by rail. Indeed it was not unknown for there to be 300 fishing boats in the harbour with 400-500 handcarts standing by on the quay to handle the catches. Small wonder, therefore, that in 1889 the Sutton Harbour Company secured an Act of Parliament giving them permission to build a new, covered, fish market.

The issue had been considered for years. Plymouth Corporation drew up plans for a fish market on Commercial Wharf, but the fishermen wanted to be inside the Harbour proper, inside the Piers.

With space at a premium the Company built on the bed of the harbour itself, thereby renewing existing rights in such affairs. The new location was infront of the Barbican and so, for the duration of the construction works, the Parade was used as a temporary market. This created an unfortunate side effect as there was only earth here between the cobbles, not cement.

The inevitable fish slime that was produced when the market was in operation seeped down between the cobbles and not only resulted in the generation of a dreadful smell, but also entered the storm water chamber located under the Parade and generated so much sewer gas that manhole covers were lifted! A ventilator was erected on the Parade with a gas burning lamp atop in an attempt to deal with the problem.

The white tiled end wall of the new fish market is on the far left as we look down Quay Road towards the Parade.

No sooner had the new fish market been opened — on 1 February 1896 — than the industry started to face a new challenge. Steam trawling had started in the North Sea and such was the size of the catches they were bringing in that the traditional sailing smacks were being forced out of business.

The first locally owned steam trawler was the *Reginald* and she came into Sutton Harbour the same year that the new fish market — curiously enough built in the style of a steam railway station — came into operation. With a red funnel abaft the wheelhouse; it was not long before she had been joined by a handful of other locally owned (Chant & Paddon) steam trawlers.

The move did not, however, mark new peaks in the fishing trade in and out of the harbour. On the contrary, there was, in the short term, a noticeable decline as the industry became concentrated in a smaller number of larger ports.

Top: *The new quay leading to the fish market.* Bottom: Underneath the canopy.

Looking across from Quay Road towards the China House with the tower of St John Sutton on Plym breaking the skyline.

1890: The Watch House, Admiral McBride, Seaman's Bethel, Brunswick Hotel, North Country Pink and the Great Western Railway Receiving Office.

Described in 1880 by one writer as an 'historic but odoriferous neighbourhood,' an attempt was made to deal with part of the problem a couple of years later, when, in 1882, John Pethick, the local builder and entrepreneur, dredged more than 30,000 tons of sewage from the harbour bed ... and estimated that there was almost as much again left.

The area was still desperately poor, congested, full of factories, fumes and fish. Nevertheless it wasn't without its charms and visitors, as another 1880s account testifies: 'At five in the morning the cafés are already open and the fishermen have collected freshly baked loaves from the bakery. A few policemen, anxious to be off their beats approach ... the street sweepers are industriously brooming and a tramp appears from somewhere, glad that the night has gone ... presently the sails of the trawlers begin to unfurl and nets are hauled down. Only three or four donkey carts have yet arrived, backed to the edge of the pavement that has to serve as a fish market. Some foreign skippers arrive, bent on an early drink.

'At the Dolphin it is heard that there has just been a catch of some 26,000 mackerel the day before. There is a ringing of bells which token that sales are commencing. Throughout the morning the coffee houses and drink shops have plenty of customers.' (WF 9 May 1884)

Most of those customers, it would appear, worked or lived locally, but in 1891, after the great number of improvements that had taken place on the Hoe to promote Plymouth as a Holiday Resort, it was announced that the Council had 'authorised the erection of memorials commemorating the departure of the Mayflower from Plymouth, and the battle between the Roundheads and Cavaliers at Freedom Fields.' (WMN 10 September 1891)

One can but speculate as to why, after all this time, it was now felt appropriate to mark such occasions, but in the case of the former it was almost certainly the visit of the Mayor of Plymouth, John Thomas Bond, to Plymouth, Massachusetts in July 1891. During that trip, 'when all that is of interest at Pilgrim Plymouth was reverently sought for by the Mayor.' (WMN 18 July 1891)

It must have become obvious that Plymouth had nothing to mark the event on the other side of the Atlantic and a subsequent visit of some American delegates to Plymouth, later that same month, doubtless accelerated the gesture.

The visit, 'in memory of the men of the Mayflower' saw 'special services conducted in many of the Congregational Chapels in the Three Towns. Several of the American ministers occupied the pulpits, and the references to the early life and thoughts of the Pilgrim Fathers were very numerous.

'Two days later the delegates were entertained on board a steamer, chartered by the Congregational Union of the Three Towns. They left the West Hoe Pier at ten o'clock, when a trip was made to the Breakwater, Saltash Bridge, and other points of interest.' (WMN 29 July 1891).

A luncheon followed in the Union Chapel Congregational Hall. The Mayor and Mayoress of Plymouth, Mr and Mrs John Thomas Bond, were present and among the formalities there was a toast of: 'The Queen and the President of the American Republic.

'Dr Whitton, of New York, said one of his ancestors was on the Mayflower, and ... it was a gratifying reflection to him that he, the descendant in the 8th generation, had been by the most singular operation of Providence, so highly privileged as to also share the hospitality of a Baptist who was no other than the chief official of Plymouth. There had,' he added, 'only been three really famous ships in the world — Noah's Ark, the Argo, and the Mayflower [applause].' (ibid)

The Mayflower Stone, created thanks to the historian RN Worth and Mayor JT Bond.

Top: *Teat's Hill and Queen Anne Battery.* Bottom: *Two steamers, one of them the Oreston & Turnchapel Steamship Co.'s Nick O'Time at the West Pier c.1890.*

As far as Plymouth and many other parts of the world are concerned, there are, of course, far more than three famous ships.

In New Zealand the *Tory*, a pioneer ship in the colonization of that country, is regarded in every bit as high esteem as the *Mayflower*.

Edward Gibbon Wakefield, the founder of the New Zealand Company was on board when the humble vessel left Plymouth in the second year of Victoria's reign.

On 25 January 1840 the Plymouth Company of New Zealand was formed by a number of local merchants, notably Thomas Gill (the West Hoe/Millbay developer) and Thomas Woollcombe. Together they purchased 60,000 acres from the New Zealand Company, with whom they soon merged, and in November 1840 they sent out their first settlers — 64 adults and 70 children — in the *William Bryan*.

Over the next year or so they sent another five ships with an overall total of 897 settlers, mainly from Devon and Cornwall and New Plymouth was founded on the North Island.

The biggest boon to local emigration though came in 1847 when the Government took over Elphinstone and Baltic wharves and the old Lambhay Victualling Yard as their emigration depot.

Victualling operations had been moved around to the then newly built Royal William Yard in the 1830s. Although still owned by the Ordnance Board, Thomas Gill is shown as being in possession of this site in 1845 and doubtless it had already served for some years as an emigration base.

At first equipped with 500 berths (later increased to 1,118), Elphinstone was the scene of great activity: in 1847, 26 vessels sailed from Plymouth carrying 1,730 emigrants. The following year the figures more than trebled and in 1849, 109 ships left here for Australia bearing over 14,000 emigrants. There were also a further 21 ships that sailed from here that year destined for other colonies — half of them bound for Canada.

The Irish potato famine of 1847, the arrival of the railways in Plymouth in 1849, the discovery of gold in Australia in 1851, and the general state of the local rural economy, all had their impact on the drive for emigration — particularly if, as previously mentioned, you were a married couple, under 35, in which case you could claim free passage to the New World.

Not all of them settled successfully, but millions of them — around two-thirds of them — did.

*The old Lambhay Victualling buildings on Commercial Wharf and Elphinstone.
Inset: Entrance to the Cattewater.*

Above: *The new landing stage at Phoenix Wharf.* Inset right: *Enamel advert for Peek Frean biscuits. George Frean founded his business at the King's Bakehouse, Commercial Wharf.* Right: *Percy Pearce.*

Meanwhile, on 10 September 1895, just along from the Emigration Depot (which by this time had moved and the buildings had been refashioned as the Government Torpedo Depot to accommodate explosives), a new and 'much-needed' public landing-stage was created just off another of the old Victualling Yard buildings — Phoenix Wharf.

Cornish-born Percy Trevarthian Pearce (of the law firm Bond, Pearce & Bickle) was Chairman of the Landing Stage Committee that had driven the project. A keen yachtsman, Percy was also, like his business partner JT Bond, a prominent local Councillor.

The main rationale for the new facility was that it would 'relieve the Barbican of much of the present congested traffic, and to some extent enable the boatmen to recover the position they had lost since the steamers had been running up and down the Cattewater.' (WMN 14 October 1891)

Not all of the old Victualling Yard buildings, incidentally, underwent such major changes of use. After the Navy moved out of what had been the King's Bakery, George Frean, a miller from Ashburton, moved in and with Messrs Dawe and Serpell, two flour millers from Drake's Mill (which originally stood on the site of Sherwell Church), started what was destined to become a well-known biscuit manufactory.

Frean didn't stay here however: in 1857 he moved to Bermondsey, where, with two Peek brothers, he set up the Peek, Frean Fancy Biscuit Company. Frean's departure was followed by Robert Coad Serpell taking over the Commercial Wharf business, although, in the last year or so the Serpell biscuit business also moved east, to Reading.

Another victualling-related business operating from Commercial Road with waterside premises on Commercial Wharf, is the Italian wine-importing business of the Teglio brothers: 'The first business for the supply of the genuine wines of Italy in the West of England.' The Teglio brothers had been 'largely encouraged by the kind commendation and patronage of numerous private families, in addition to leading restaurants, clubs and hotels, who have found the wines of Italy of the merit described and to a great extent superior to the wines of other countries.'

So ran a few lines from their 1894 publicity material. Other quotes included: 'Italian wines were first exhibited on anything like an important scale in this country at the Health Exhibition a few years ago, and since then they have risen considerably in popular favour (Colonies & India).

'When a wine is not artificially sweetened, we have a beverage of great utility as a stimulant, and which does the very minimum of harm. A population that drinks only such wines rarely produces a dipsomaniac.' (The Lancet)

Top: Commercial Wharf. Bottom: Men at work in Teglio's No.3 bottling cellar. Right: Teglio advert from 1894.

Castle Street in the 1890s after it had been cleaned up.

One place where, earlier this century, you may well have encountered the odd dipsomaniac was just up from Commercial Road, in Castle Street.

'Castle Street or "The Rag," in which every house was formerly an inn and every inn a brothel, had mitigated its character as the result of the courageous interposition of the Rev. Francis Barnes, who more than once entered its Infernos when nude men and women were dancing causing the furies to decamp before his stern rebuke, and some landlords to disappear without even removing their furniture.' (Whitfeld 1899)

'Without check or remonstrance, pigs and fowls were bred in cellars and gardens, most houses were without water, and there were no facilities for removing offal. White's Lane, Stoke's Lane, Pin's Lane, and Garrison Lane were thick with filthy accumulations; few of the backlets were provided with closets, washhouses or drying places; and drains were considered a doubtful luxury.'

'Disgusting as were even the scenes by day, a second community rendered the district hideous by night a population of the destitute and dissolute, who inhaled their own pestilential odours, and vanished with the sunrise.' (ibid)

Should this sound exaggerated, a 'very faithful but by no means flattering picture of the town,' as it appeared in 1852, was drawn by Robert Rawlinson (one of the first inspectors appointed in the wake of the 1848 Public Health Act).

'Rawlinson describes nearly every house and shop as having an independent style of its own; the macadamised streets as very dirty in wet weather and very dusty in dry; the old back streets as narrow, crooked, and steep, with narrow passages leading into dirtier and still more crowded courts.' (Worth 1890)

'One privy serves the whole court, and this is usually filthy; the cess pool full, overflowing and the foetid refuse stagnant over the surface. An external standpipe, the water on only for one hour in twenty four, supplies water to an entire court with many tenants; tubs, mugs, pots, pans, and troughs being placed in the yard, on the stairs, landings, or in the filthy rooms, to absorb all the deleterious gases of the place. Within, the furniture accords with the premises; it is old, rotten, broken, and ruinous. One room serves for a family of father, mother, and children — not infrequently grown up sons and daughters. Dogs and fowl inhabit the same apartment, and, in some instances, ten human beings.

Already a partial ruin — note the missing roof tiles on the left of the structure — this curious dwelling at the bottom of Lambhay Street is thought to have been constructed with stonework from the town's medieval, four-towered castle.

'Originally many of the houses now in ruins were erected as residences for the nobility and gentry of the town; but from being the abodes of those possessing wealth they now give partial shelter to the improvident, the vagrant, the vicious and the unfortunate. The quaint carving on the stonework looks out of place; the walls are half in ruins; the gables are shattered, and foul weather stains of damp blotch the surface. Within, matters are even worse; the rooms are now divided and subdivided on every floor; the staircase is darkened; its massive handrail and carved balusters are crippled and broken; the once firm stairs are now rickety and dangerous; the stucco-finished plastering is blackened and in holes.' *(Rawlinson 1852)*

Attempts were made to improve matters. There was a major drive to improve sanitation across the Three Towns, and as some of the improvements became effective, so there was a, largely short-lived, exercise in street re-naming: 'Castle Rag, alias Damnation Alley, alias Silver Street the last named representing an unsuccessful attempt to disguise its tattered morality.' *(Whitfeld 1899)*

New Street was another thoroughfare to have a number of names over the years — among them Rag Street and Greyfriars Street.

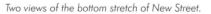

Looking down one of the town's narrowest inhabited thoroughfares — Castle Dyke Lane.

Two views of the bottom stretch of New Street.

*Pin Lane: These 'quaint little houses had become very dilapidated, and were very insanitary; consequently, their removal was necessary.
Nevertheless one cannot but regret that so picturesque bit of old Plymouth could not have been preserved.' (Wright 1901)*

The early part of the Nineteenth Century saw a number of substantial warehouses erected in New Street, several of them to house the booty plundered by British ships in the Napoleonic Wars.

In recent years they have been used by a variety of enterprises. One of them, running along the eastern side of Castle Dyke Lane, belongs to Collier & Co. Primarily Wine & Spirit Merchants; the business was established by Jonathan Collier back in 1676, making them one of the longest running concerns in the area. Members of the family also became significantly involved in the affairs of the area with both father, son John, and Richard Collier serving the town as MPs, while William Collier, another son, served six years as a councillor.

The Collier's main business premises was in Southside Street, where it was founded. It stood just two doors down from the splendid Tudor building at the bottom of Pin Lane, a building that it is said was once owned by the only one of Drake's officers to have lost his life in the encounter with the Spanish Armada — Captain Lucas Cocke.

Another building that dates back to the days of Queen Elizabeth is Fone's Bakery. Although it is but one of more than a half-a-dozen bakeries in this street in recent years, this remarkable bread and biscuit shop has been in the same family since at least 1597, at which point we believe it was a free-standing property rather like the nearby Island House.

Southside Street is undoubtedly the busiest of retail thoroughfares in the ancient heart of Plymouth, sporting all manner of goods and services, as well as several public houses, among them the Royal Oak, the Queen's Arms (formerly the Plymouth Arms but renamed shortly after Victoria came to the throne), the Maritime, the Custom's House Tavern ('No Women Allowed') and the Navy — 'Table d'hote daily at 1pm and hearty welcome to all captains visiting the port,' states their promotional material, 'Master mariners, passengers and families,' it adds, 'will find every accommodation and comfort'.

Top left: Collier's on the corner of Castle Dyke Lane and New Street. Right: Rear of Collier's store. Above: Fone Warren's bakery in Southside Street c.1895.

Southside Street c.1880. The buildings to the left of the gable-ended Tudor building, including the Albion on the corner of Pin Lane opposite, were pulled down soon afterwards. The Queen's Arms — erstwhile Plymouth Arms — is on the far right and Collier's is two to the left of it.

58 Southside Street: Business premises of Pitts, Son & King: Merchants and Maltsters.

Doubtless they would also have found Plymouth Gin, another long-established brand, bottled and distilled at the other end of the street.

Established by Coates & Co. at the end of the Eighteenth Century, the business grew impressively during the course of the Nineteenth Century. In 1870 the company decided to capitalise on the, albeit mythical, notion of the order of the Blackfriars and include the figure of a friar on their bottle labels. The distillery sits on the corner of Southside Street and Blackfriars Lane, but there were only ever Greyfriars in this neighbourhood, and it has been suggested that stonework from the original Greyfriars' establishment, notably door frames and window mullions, have been incorporated into the fabric of the building, which predates the setting up of the distillery.

Winners of a prize medal at the 1884 International Health Exhibition, Coates' Plymouth Gin had, for a time, competition from another local distillery, in Vauxhall Street.

And, oddly enough, that same year, 1884, they were awarded an injunction prohibiting anyone from selling or passing off any gin not of their manufacture as Coates & Co.'s Plymouth Gin. Another case in 1887 revealed that there were no less than three other firms in the town manufacturing gin that was commonly known as Plymouth gin.

An 1890 advertisement for 'another' Plymouth gin.

ORIGINAL PLYMOUTH GIN
Prize Medal, Health Exhibition, 1884.
ESTABLISHED 1793.
Messrs. Coates & Co.
OF THE
BLACK FRIARS DISTILLERY,
PLYMOUTH,
Are the ONLY Distillers of the
ORIGINAL PLYMOUTH GIN
Protected by Perpetual Injunction in
Chancery of 1st March, 1884, and
10th February, 1887.

Scenes from the Coates' Plymouth Gin distillery in Southside Street.
Left: *An 1890s advert.* Middle: *Medal from 1884* Far right: *An early label*

David Laing's imposing Custom House overlooking the Parade.

While a number of new developments have appeared in this area during the course of the present century, few if any, have been as striking as the new Custom House.

Built over a number of years using French prisoners of war, who also worked on the Royal William Victualling Yard and Dartmoor Prison, where many of the prisoners were housed, the building was completed in 1820 and first occupied by the Department in 1823.

That was the year, incidentally, that Parliament decided to end the situation whereby there were separate boards of customs and excise for England, Scotland and Ireland, creating instead one Board of Excise for the whole of the United Kingdom.

Designed by David Laing 'the edifice was erected by Mr Ball under the direction of D Laing, Esq. The front is built of granite with a colonnade of five arches supported by rusticated piers of the same material. Inside, the staircase, likewise of granite, leads to the long-room, a commodious and spacious apartment for the dispatch of general business, adjoining which are the comptroller's and collector's offices.' (*Guide to Plymouth 1821*)

'On the ground floor are the offices of the principal surveyor, tide surveyor, landing waites, searchers, &c.' (*Wright 1879*).

The cost of the scheme was £8,000, and perhaps it should have been more, as one of the local firms involved, carpenters and glaziers Gribble & Hellyer, went bankrupt before the building was completed, complaining that they had been poorly paid.

A more recent development, has seen Enoch Tope move his business from Hoe Street to the Parade. Having started out as a cook on ocean-going-liners, Enoch decided to set up as a pastry cook and soon had a thriving trade catering for children's parties. As well as supplying cakes for functions, the enterprising Enoch also supplied cutlery and linen. Before long, tents and marquees in which to hold the parties were available for sale or hire.

Very quickly it seems the tent manufacturing became a bigger part of the business than the cake making — hence the decision to move. Thus it was that his son, Richard Brooking Tope, came to be trading on the Parade as a 'baker and marquee contractor.' Enoch was still involved and with Richard's keen business acumen, the company grew quickly. Tarpaulins, cloths, flags — 'by appointment to the Principal Yacht Clubs' — all became part of the offer, as this has become one of many successful manufactories around the harbour.

RB Tope: maker of marquees, tents and flags.

Vauxhall Quay looking across to the corner of Vauxhall Street and Woolster Street.

Sutton Harbour has very much come into its own during the Nineteenth Century, its success largely underpinning the success of the town itself off the back of the Industrial Revolution.

Another excellent case study is that of Messrs Pitts, Son & King whose offices we have already seen in Southside Street.

Established in 1804 this house 'is one which has conspicuously contributed to the advancement and development of the malting and fertilising trades of Western England, and in connection with these highly important branches of British trade, it continues to occupy a position of distinction and repute.

'The immense premises occupied are suitably equipped, and the capabilities of the firm's new crushing and grinding machinery are unequalled in the West of England. Large steamers lay alongside the warehouses in the Docks, and at Sutton Harbour, to unload and load their huge and costly cargoes.

'The resources of the establishment are devoted to the preparation and supply of fertilising agents of every description — potash (kainit), nitrate of soda, guanos, vitriolised bones, superphosphates, special manures for barley, oats, grass, potatoes, etc., whilst the feeding stuffs embrace grain of all kinds, cakes, crushed maize, beans, barley meal, peas, oats, feeding malt, compound horse cattle and pig foods, bran, flaked barley, compound cake, &c., their linseed cake (Pearson's) being warranted to contain at least 96 per cent of purity.

'At considerable outlay, a new plant has been laid down for malt roasting and torrifying barley, and a large double-floor kiln (Herman's patent), with a kiln-drying capacity, unrivalled in the neighbourhood, has recently been constructed. The firm's operations are obviously conducted upon quite an exceptional scale. They are the largest manufacturers of malt in the west, and are also direct importers of grain, manure, and cakes, the aggregate turnover considerably exceeding that of any similar trading concern in these counties.'

Above: *Pitts' premises in Stillman Place.* Right: *Stores and Mills. Telephone No.92.*

Above: *Busy scene on North Quay (note the Co-op premises, they first opened stores there in the 1880s).*
Right: *SS Newbiggin from the railway turntable. Launched in 1883, the Newbiggin collided with and sank the British screw steamship The City of Rotterdam in thick fog off the Eddystone Reef in 1900.*

Sutton Harbour has undoubtedly made an enormous contribution to the economy of the Three Towns. It would, however have been even greater had the plans of the celebrated Great Western Railways engineer Isambard Kingdom Brunel come to fruition in the 1840s. At the beginning of that decade Sutton Harbour was already vibrant. Although most of the western side of the pool had been developed, Coxside, to the east, was still largely rural as was most of Millbay.

In the summer of 1838 when the *Sirius* beat Brunel's *Great Western* marking the first regular Transatlantic ferry service, she moored in the Cattewater and her cargo of mail and newspapers was dropped on the Barbican steps. However, it was only a little over a year later that Thomas Gill, soon to be MP for the town (1841-46), announced plans to build a landing-pier at Millbay. Gill, had a financial interest in Sutton Harbour, but an even bigger one in Millbay. He had also, as you will recall, quarried away much of Drake's Hoe (and made enough money in the process to rent Drake's former home of Buckland Abbey).

Gill's 500-foot-long pier, completed in 1844, made Millbay more viable than ever as a port of call — it could now receive vessels of up to 3,000 tons — and although Sutton Harbour was already connected to the South Devon Railway (a horse-drawn affair of which Gill was Chairman), the prospect of linking with the steam railway network was the real prize.

In the event it was the Admiralty that determined the outcome. They didn't want to see the lock gates at Sutton Harbour as proposed by Brunel as that would render it less effective as a harbour of refuge for them, whereas there was no such objection to the Millbay proposals that were deposited at the same time.

Undeterred, a smaller-scale project was drawn up for Sutton Pool, by the newly formed Sutton Harbour Improvement Company. The organisation superseded an earlier body and included several new directors, among them John Alger and William Burnell, who had soap and chemical companies at Coxside, and John Pope who had a substantial sail and rope business at Teat's Hill — all on the eastern side of the harbour.

Gradually the new organisation grew and in 1876, the year that the London & South Western Railway eventually reached North Quay, the Improvement Company acquired the right to purchase: 'all the water, soil and pool of Sutton situate near the Borough of Plymouth.'

Top: *Colonel Jory's Almhouses, erected in 1703, that stood at the end of what became Sutton Road.* Bottom: *Eden Brothers Coal and Coke Merchants, Sutton Road, established in the 1860s. 'Large stocks of coal regularly kept, including Wallsend, Ballo, Silkstone, steam coals, baker's nuts, and other good classes ...' Note the proximity of the ship's mast.*

A fine example of Tudor architecture in Higher Street — gone before the end of the century.

While there may not have been much work in terms of the built environment on the eastern banks of Sutton Pool prior to the Nineteenth Century, there was a not insignificant amount on the northern fringes, but that too has recently been undergoing change.

'It is not long since, that in Higher Street, on the north side of Exeter Street, and Lower Street on the south side of the same street there could be seen numerous picturesque houses such as those on this page. In common with nearly all the old streets of Plymouth the hand of the destroyer has been busy, and these fine gabled houses have been demolished to give place to newer and less picturesque dwellings.

'In this way old Plymouth is vanishing and new Plymouth is arising in all the glory of new bricks and ugly stucco to the disgust of the lovers of the picturesque on the one hand, but to the joy of the utilitarian on the other.' *(Wright 1901)*

Higher Street, long ago known as Hawk Street, was for centuries the highest, in the sense of being the most northerly, principal street of the town that ran in an east-west direction and, being on the outskirts of town, was once very fashionable.

Like so many of Plymouth's old streets however, it's character has changed significantly in the Nineteenth Century. The junction with North Street originally marked the western end of Higher Street towards which this view takes us: at the other end it terminated at its meeting with Exeter Street.

Lower Street, running parallel to Exeter Street, sits just below that.

Narrower than Higher Street, Lower Street's fortunes has fallen lower than most in the Nineteenth Century and at one time there were over 500 people living in fewer than 30 houses. At that time the national average of people per household was about 5.5, in Plymouth generally the figure was a little over nine, while in Lower Street itself it was nearer 20 with at least 40 rooms sleeping four or more.

The insanitary conditions created by the overcrowding in the street took an obvious toll on the residents and more than one in five of the women living in Lower Street over the age of 16 were widows.

Another, even more ancient, piece of our architectural heritage has disappeared recently too — the last surviving fragments and buildings of the medieval Carmelite Friary that gave way to the London & South Western Railway Station in the 1870s.

Curiously enough this too had become more of a den of iniquity rather than antiquity as a most wonderful account in the *South Devon Monthly Museum* of 1835 bears witness.

The author, having borrowed a most ancient hat, an old hunting-coat and a pair of fisherman's boots with only one sole, spent a very lively, and what he deemed to be very typical Saturday night there.

Tom Hynes presided over the proceedings and among the many guests, anything up to four dozen of them, were dealers in cabbage nets and matches ('often blinds to cover the more lucrative occupation of thieving'), bellow makers, knife grinders, and umbrella renovators ('generally gypsies'), wandering Italians (men in command of gangs of boys who 'perambulate the streets with an organ, a monkey, a white mouse or some other means of amusement'), thimble riggers and prod-in-the-loop boys (gambling con men), solicitors and booksellers.

If the last two mentioned sound almost respectable remember these solicitors were the sort who wrote begging letters and the booksellers sold scandal sheets, typically accounts of 'bloody murders, accidents, offences &c.'

Most of these characters would have slept here too, in straw beds laid out on the floor with no more than six inches between them. 'Bedclothes there were none, each traveller sleeping in the habiliments which decorate him by day. As for the great Saturday night feast itself, this was eaten without the aid of knives and forks, off upturned barrels and uneven tables and it consisted of fish, fowl, ham, beef, cheese, turnips, onions, bread and an ample tin cauldron holding about a wheelbrarrow full of potatoes. For libations at dinner each guest was provided with a pewter pot of Scott's XXX ale.'

'After supper came brandy, the best that was ever smuggled from "Guarnsy" island. Towards midnight Tom Hynes slipped off his chair under one of the tables while Jack o'Diamonds and Billy Brown turned to for a bruising match, whereupon the writer thought fit to evaporate into thin air.'

Friary Gate, the last fragment and one-time entrance to the Carmelite Friary above North Quay.

Standing almost directly opposite the old Friary Gate is the Exeter Street premises of Messrs. James Hawker & Co., Wine & Spirit Merchants (they have another base in Bedford Street). 'Situated midway in Exeter Street (contiguous to Sutton Pool, and, as a natural consequence conveniently situated for shipping), the business was founded several generations ago, by the present proprietors' ancestors, and as importers of wines and liqueurs they have advanced in influence and importance of connection consistently with the improved conditions of wine growing and shipping.

'Their famous "Sloe Gin" ("Pedlar Brand") is well known, and need not be confounded with the cordial commonly sold under that name. It is prepared, we are informed, with the greatest care, only from the very best materials, and has already obtained great reputation among hunting men, who recognise it as one of the best liqueurs with which to fill a flask. When we say that the it is supplied to HRH the Duke of Edinburgh, KG (from whom Messrs. James Hawker & Co. hold, as wine merchants, a special appointment), no doubt can be entertained as to the excellence of the brand; and the assertion the trade acknowledge it to be the finest in the market, derives ample support from the fact that the demand for it is increasing every day from all parts of England and of the world, large quantities being exported to various quarters of the globe.' (Wright 1894)

Made to a secret sixteenth-century recipe, and only in Plymouth, this is undoubtedly one of the town's most famous businesses, a fact that is enhanced locally in the naming of the thoroughfare that it sits on the corner of, on Exeter Street, and which connects it but a short distance to the quayside — Hawker's Avenue.

'Meanwhile, among the notable business houses in Plymouth, whose present marked degrees of mercantile prosperity stand not only as evidence of past energy, activity, and honourable method, but also as an earnest of augmented success and enhanced reputation in days to come, the old-established business now under the vigorous control of Mr Richard Bray is evidently deserving of a place in these pages devoted to the promotion of commercial enterprise and effort in this ancient town.' (ibid)

Described as a wholesale general warehouseman, Richard Bray occupies two large warehouses in Buckwell Street and here he stores: 'all kinds of haberdashery goods of the newest and most approved designs, while the general stock includes … confectionery, tea, coffee, chocolate, chicory, cornflour, spices, mustard, seeds, pills, blue, black lead, starch, washing powder, soap, stationery, toys, brushes, combs, matches, cigars, cigarettes, pipes, clocks etc., together with an infinite variety of miscellaneous goods coming under the category of sundries, duly enumerated in their catalogue.' (ibid)

Top: *Hawkers Wine Merchants, on the corner of Hawker's Avenue and Exeter Street.*
Bottom: *Bray's warehouses on the corner of Buckwell Street and Holycross Lane.*

Buckwell Street looking up towards Treville Street. Richard Bray's warehouses are on the far right, with the cobbled entrance to Holycross Lane running off to the right.

The corner of Buckwell Street and Looe Street c.1890, the buildings on the left are not long for this world

At the southern end of Buckwell Streeet stands Looe Street, once one of the most fashionable street in the town, with Drake and Trelawney among those who had houses here.

Originally all of these fine residences had substantial gardens but, over the years, these came to be filled in with small cottages for household servants and workmen, a pattern typical of many of the older, grander streets of Plymouth. By the mid-Nineteenth Century Looe Street had become infilled to such an extent that it had become one of the town's congested slum areas.

'The ground rises abruptly, and slippery half worn limestone steps lead to houses more ruinous and more crowded than those fronting the street,' wrote Robert Rawlinson in his 1853 report for the General Board of Health.

There was a fundamental problem: 'In almost every centre of population the demand for houses far exceeds the supply, and families are crowded together in buildings that are altogether inadequate for the occupants. With the demand for houses comes an increase in the rent, and poor people are driven to occupy rooms which have not the ordinary conveniences of domestic life. In every large town there are hundreds of families who have to be content with a single room. What chance of health or happiness in such conditions? Of course, so long as poverty exists there will always be a certain class driven to live in these wretched tenements; and, unfortunately, they never strive to improve their position, preferring to waste their substance in gambling and in the public-house rather than spend the money they get on comfortable habitation.' (WMN 1891)

By this stage something was being done in the wake of Mayor JT Bond's slum tour of the area the previous year. Soon all the north side of Looe Street had been cleared, along with almost all of the neighbouring How Street and in their place the local authority were, for the first time, providing municipal accommodation: 'two, three and four roomed dwellings were' we read in February 1898, 'soon to be built, and there will be a total accommodation here for 500 people.' Unfortunately, the article went on to state that: 'the number displaced by the scheduling of condemned areas in this district is 813.'

Whatever the imbalance caused by this, the new blocks of Artisans' Dwellings were opened in 1898 in the Mayoralty of Alderman John Pethick, who had himself been involved in providing supplementary accommodation here for the working classes.

Top: A similar view to that on the opposite page: Above left: Looking west almost at the top of Looe Street, the old Guildhall just visible in the distance. Above right: The bottom end of Looe Street, with everything on the right destined to disappear. All three images circa 1890.

Hicks Lane, running south off Looe Street.

One of the best examples of how the erstwhile garden areas had become built up is in the narrow thoroughfare tucked in between No.25 and No.27 Looe Street — Hicks Lane.

Remarkably it even has an even smaller 'street', Looe Place, running at right angles off it, creating an extra set of postal addresses between Looe Street and Stillman Street.

If Drake might have been turning in his watery grave at the thought of what had happened at West Hoe, what would he have made of the decline of those parts of Plymouth he had known — and owned a substantial amount of property in?

In his day the two great Monasteries more or less marked the north and south extent of the town and within that area almost all of Plymouth lived, the rich and the poor.

By the middle of the Nineteenth Century most of those who could afford to had moved out as our roads and our transport made it easier and, given the boom in urban population, desirable.

For the once-grand properties they left behind there was a similar pattern, we have already alluded to it, but perhaps the one structure that epitomises the sorry sequence more than any other is Palace Court.

'Palace Court, entered by an arched doorway, is situated in Catte Street, not far from the Old Guildhall, and is at the present time, so far removed from anything palatial in appearance, or in fact, that it has simply become the residence — being let off in separate floors and rooms — of people of the very lowest ranks of society. It is, indeed, a place to be but once visited, and that, a visit of but short duration. Still, putting aside all feelings of disgust at the modes of living of its denizens, or of the filth and squalor of the place it is worth a visit, and some few interesting features will repay examination — especially a carved corbel on the landing of one of the principal staircases. Of this 'Palace Court' denuded of an excrescence, which has been built up in the quadrangle, and so cuts off some portion even of the little amount of free air the inhabitants formerly had to breath, we give an engraving ...'

That graphic description of Palace Court appeared in Llewellynn Jewitt's *History of Plymouth*, published in 1873. Within seven years this 'venerable house ... the most picturesque house in the town' had been pulled down.

Palace Court with 'excrescence'. John Paynter's fifteenth-century home — here he entertained 16-year-old Catherine of Arragon, en route to London to marry Henry VII's eldest son Arthur.

Stillman Street showing, second left, the birthplace of John Kitto.

Following the demolition of Palace Court an impressive new school, Palace Court Board School, was erected on the site. At the opening ceremony, on Tuesday 31 May 1881, the Rev. T Whitby, a member of the school board, remarked: 'that among certain sections of the community they had heard loud cries against the demolition of old Palace Court, but he thought that those who wished such a wretched and dilapidated structure to stand should have been made to live in it,' to which there was laughter and applause.

'He was very glad indeed to think this spot had been cleared and such a handsome school erected upon the site — (hear, hear).'

The Reverend then: 'alluded to the provision of dual desks in their new school, which had been found to give general satisfaction wherever tried.' (WDM 1 June 1881)

The proceedings had actually been opened by the Chairman of the School Board, the Rev. Frederick Anthony. A former pupil at the Western College, Mutley, 49-year-old Anthony returned to Plymouth, and to Western College, six years later, after graduating from London University, taking up a position as Classical and Mathematical Tutor.

In 1871 he was elected to the inaugural School Board, appointed under the terms of the 1870 Education Acts and in 1877 he became Chairman of the Board.

At the opening of Palace Court he gave a brief account of the work of the Board since its creation stating that 'the Palace Court School constituted the seventh pile of buildings the School Board had put up since its election. The Treville Street Schools, were not far distant from the spot they were assembled upon, were the first erected by the Board. These were followed by the schools in Castle Street and Sutton Road, then Wolsden Street, Mount Street, and Oxford Street School, and now Palace Court. Another school, King Street, had been purchased by the Board, and was under their guidance.

'Referring to attendance of the schools in the town, he mentioned that in 1870, just before the School Board was elected, there were upon the registers of the various schools of Plymouth, the names of 7,125 children, with an average attendance of 5,000: but in 1880, there were upon the school registers throughout the town, including voluntary and Board Schools, the names of 10,799 children, not far short of an increase of 4,000 while they had an average attendance of 8,343 — (applause).'

Rev FE Anthony

The school was intended to take the boys of Stillman Street and the girls and infants from Batter Street Schools. The school offered accommodation for 247 boys, 288 girls and 257 infants.

The Mayor, prior to officially opening the new buildings, mentioned that he'd received a letter from one of the senior magistrates, W Luscombe, who was unable to attend the event on medical grounds, and was keen to flag up the historical associations enjoyed by the site.

The Chairman later pointed out that Mr Luscombe had, to everyone's 'gratifying and pleasing surprise,' gifted the school a painting of Old Palace Court.

Another local worthy unable to attend that evening was Thomas Pitts who had recently erected a tablet 'within hail of that place, to preserve the memory of that worthy Plymothian John Kitto, who was born in that street.

Kitto, who became one of the foremost biblical scholars in the country with an international reputation, had had an interesting early career. Born in Stillman Street (earlier known as Catte Street) in 1804, he had little formal schooling but developed an early love for books. While aged 13, working for his father on a building site in Batter Street — his father was a mason — he fell 35 feet to the ground when carrying slates up a ladder.

For two weeks he lay unconscious and when he finally recovered he found that he had lost his hearing, a disability that ultimately was to throw him even further into the literary world.

By the time he died, in 1854, John Kitto was widely regarded as one of Plymouth's foremost nineteenth-century scholars. In 1880, or thereabouts, his birthplace was demolished and a new malthouse for Pitts, Son & King (previously illustrated) was erected on the site, hence the erection of the tablet.

John Kitto.

Salutation Inn demolished c1898 in Stillman Street (it had also been known as Seven Stars Lane).

The Plymouth Co-operative Society's first ever Plymouth store in Catte Street.

The birth of John Kitto is by no means the only significant birth to have taken place in Catte Street, or Stillman Street as it became known, in the Nineteenth Century.

On 2 February 1860 a Society was born in No.14 Catte Street — the Plymouth Co-operative Society. One of the prime movers in the enterprise was 45-year-old local shoemaker, Charles Goodanew, who, on Christmas Day 1859, read extracts from George Jacob Holyoake's *Self Help by the People — History of the Rochdale Pioneers*.

Listening to him were two local craftsmen, John Slade and John Shovel. All three were unhappy with the world as they saw it. Plymouth was overcrowded: the population of around 60,000 was almost four times what it had been when Goodanew was born. Sanitation was poor, so too were the majority of the population. Food was expensive and all too often adulterated: typically aluminium sulphate was used to bulk up bread, white lead was added to flour, copper sulphate to bottled fruit and jam, iron sulphate to tea and beer, lead to wine and cider, red lead to coffee, ground glass to sugar and lead sulphate and bisulphate of mercury to sugared confectionery and chocolate.

Such wicked tampering over time brought on chronic gastritis and often fatal food poisoning.

Such practices were widespread. In 1877 the Local Government Board found that almost a quarter of all the milk they inspected had been watered down or bulked out with chalk ... or both.

Charles Goodanew had many mouths to feed, although, tragically, four of his nine children had already died — three of them without reaching their third birthdays. His eldest daughter, however, had already married and was six months pregnant.

Something had to be done. The example of the Rochdale Pioneers showed that by uniting, subscribing a shilling, and working together, they could perhaps buy quality goods themselves and sell them direct to people like themselves safe in the knowledge that the produce hadn't been tampered with. Furthermore, they could also ensure that any trading surpluses could be re-invested.

Any profit could be issued in the form of a dividend, allocated in accordance with how much each co-operator had spent in the Co-operative store.

That first store was in one of three properties owned by John Slade, in Catte Street and it was agreed that the fledgling society should pay the princely sum of one shilling and ten pence a week for the privilege.

Map showing Catte Street running between High Street and Stillman Street. Inset: Charles Goodanew, a founder of the Plymouth Co-operative Society

Far left: *Looking up High Street toward the Napoleon Inn which stands close to the house in which Plymouth's celebrated painter Charles Locke Eastlake used to live: there is even speculation that he may have worked on his pictures of the prisoner Napoleon on board HMS Bellerophon in Plymouth Sound here in 1815.*
Left: *Further down High Street near the junction with Notte Street.*

'Few people, perhaps, who pass down High Street towards the quays realise that for centuries this old thoroughfare was the principal street of Plymouth. Long before George Street or Bedford Street were known, centuries before Union Street emerged from the marshes, the High Street of Plymouth was the very heart and centre of the famous old town. Up and down this street the brave men who helped to make up the history of Elizabethan days passed and repassed, exchanging greetings with friends and comrades and perchance, holding revel in one or other of the taverns or houses of call with which the neighbourhood abounded.

'Little do the dwellers in the now squalid tenements and crowded courts imagine that the generations of fair women and brave men lived and loved in what were in those olden days mansions, and are now the mere backwaters of the prosperous life of the modern progressive town.

'Here in what are now designated slums, lived the merchant princes and the men of light and leading of their day, and there were many prosperous traders who carried on their avocations in Plymouth's High Street.' *(Wright 1901)*

Far right: *Looking down High Street from just below the old guildhall - the properties above the horse and cart are the same as those that we see above the horse and cart in the picture on the opposite page. Meanwhile, the houses we see to the immediate right are those we see in the picture looking down the street just as the road curves around to the left.*

'It is even now picturesque, but squalor goes hand in hand with the signs of ancient dignity, and decay is visible everywhere. Nevertheless it is still High Street, and to those who are interested in it for old time's sake, it is still reminiscent of those olden Elizabethan days.

'For a time its name was changed, and it was known as Market Street, the market, or a portion of it, being carried on beneath the Old Guildhall which stood at the top; its successor, in fact, stands there still as a witness and landmark to past generations, although its character is altered. In dealing with such a subject as this, one feels that ordinary prosaic language is not sufficiently expressive; romance is in the very air, the whole neighbourhood teems with suggestions of ancient days; of vanished glory and dignity of this old street, and of those who frequented it in by gone ages.

'We can picture Drake the intrepid, whose town house was not far away, the bluff old sea dog Hawkins who probably had a house in this very street, the courtly and chivalrous Raleigh, who, on his visits to Plymouth is supposed to have lodged in Notte Street.' *(ibid)*

The erstwhile grand Elizabethan house in Notte Street, rumoured to have been a residence of Raleigh, and pulled down in the early 1880s.

'Notte Street, or Nut Street as it was sometimes called, was formerly, like all the old Plymouth streets, very narrow and not particularly straight. It was, however, graced with several fine old houses, not the least pretentious being the grand old Elizabethan mansion shown in the accompanying image. This was one of the finest specimens of Tudor architecture that the town possessed, and was a worthy example of the many ancient domestic buildings which existed up to a few years ago to show what a picturesque old town Plymouth must have been.

'What is the history of this old mansion no one can tell; tradition says that it was the residence of Sir Walter Raleigh, but that is doubtful, and there is no evidence to prove it.' *(Wright 1901)*

Despite a number of voices suggesting the building should be preserved it was swept away in the early 1880s and for once the buildings that were thrown up in its stead actually attempted to preserve something of the flavour of what had been there before.

In 1883 Messrs Bulteel & Company of the Naval Bank oversaw the creation of an imposing terrace that was to house the Plymouth Municipal Artisans' Dwellings.

Meanwhile, on the other side of the road, 'the finest house in Plymouth of the Queen Anne period is [also] in Notte Street.

'Set back from the street, the front is entirely of Portland stone, and the details are exceedingly good.

'Here lived for many years [and died] Cookworthy of china-clay and Plymouth pottery fame. Can you picture him, the quiet Quaker in his drab suit, seated in his wainscoted parlour before the fire-place with its blue and white Dutch tiles? The house is unique in its way, and nothing half so good will replace it.' *(W Hine 17 November 1882).*

Earlier that year Isaac Foot had bought the dilapidated, multi-tenanted building for £640. Foot conducted a construction business from premises on the other side of Notte Street and the building he ultimately erected in Notte Street — a Christian Mission Hall — was built directly in front of what was also known as the 'Old Mayoralty House'.

Foot also preserved the impressive sculpturing that had been above the original main front entrance to the house and had a second made with each embellishing the upper-floor, front side-windows of the two-storey Mission Hall.

Top: *The Artisans' Dwellings that were erected in 1883 in Notte Street.*
Bottom: *The former Cookworthy building, also known as the Old Mayoralty House.*

'St Andrew's Street may certainly be called one of the oldest streets of Old Plymouth. Within living memory it contained some good specimens of Tudor architecture and some of the best examples in the town. With their high gabled roofs, and projecting upper storeys, these old houses formed a picturesque feature in the street architecture of Plymouth. Modern improvements and sanitary considerations have, however, swept away nearly all that is picturesque.

'One side of this street has been entirely removed, but on the other, or west side, are still to be found some notable examples of ancient buildings, the one depicted here being the best example.' (Wright 1901)

Far left: *Looking up St Andrew Street towards Bedford Street.*
Left: *33 St Andrew Street with the sign of the Swan Hotel in the foreground.*
Above: *The corner of St Andrew Street and Abbey Place.*

One of the victims of the cull of ancient buildings on the eastern side of St Andrew Street was the Turk's Head, which stood on the corner of Higher Lane. 'Whether or not it had always been an inn has generally been a matter for conjecture. Could we trust the name we might say that the Turk's Head was a relic of the crusading days, but we fear we must not indulge in the romantic visions that fancied connection shadows forth.' *(Wright 1901)*

Harris, writing in manuscript notes written at various times during the early part of the Nineteenth Century, called it the Abbot's House, and further stated that there 'could hardly be a doubt that it is coeval with the Old Church, to which it has always belonged.' Whatever the true age of the building though and however many years it saw service as an inn, in the summer of 1861 it all came to an end — doubtless a sad one for James Stevens, one of the last licensees here, but not so for John Damerell, the first licensee of the Abbey Hotel that arose on a similar footprint.

As for St Andrew's itself, in 1825 John Foulston had drawn up plans to 'restore' the interior. The old 'unsightly galleries' were pulled down and new ones were put up but not everyone liked the outcome: 'Irreparable mischief was done, for Mr Foulston had no feeling for Gothic art' (Worth). 'Foulston applied his Gothic art with little respect for antiquity and he reduced the church to a mere shadow of itself.' *(Whitfeld)*

The dissatisfaction with Foulston's work was resolved in the 1870s when another, more major, restoration was undertaken. The galleries were removed and the interior returned to the simple open space it had originally been.

St Andrew's Church interior c.1894.

Top: *Turk's Head demolished in 1860.* Bottom: *St Andrew's Church.*

St Andrew's Church, Prysten House and, sandwiched in between, the old Workhouse. Inset: Ten years later with the Police Station at the back of the Guildhall in Catherine Street.

Foulston's 'improvements to St Andrew's were executed the year after John Hatchard arrived as the new vicar of the town's parish church in 1824, and curiously enough, Foulston's work was subsequently undone, soon after Hatchard's death in office, in 1869.'

By that time a great many other changes were afoot in this neighbourhood as the buildings at the top of Catherine Street had either been removed or were not long for this world.

Like those disappearing properties in St Andrew Street these ancient edifices were also eminently distinctive and had played key parts in the town's early history.

The Hospital of the Poor's Portion (better known latterly as the Workhouse) was completed in 1630 while the Grammar School next door, founded by the Corporation, in 1571, was built in 1615.

In 1849, however, the Guardians of the Workhouse resolved to erect a new building on land that the Hospital had been endowed with on the 'Moore Splatt north of Crosse Downs' — Greenbank.

So it was that the site of this venerable pile with its quadrangle, large Bridewell, its pound for hemp beating, its cells, dormitories, hall and numerous offices was later sold to the Corporation, in 1857, as part of the site for the proposed new Guildhall and Municipal buildings.

The following year, the Corporation Grammar School also moved out of Catherine Street (firstly to Alfred Place and the to Princess Square, in 1866, and Park Street in 1885) and that site too was cleared.

The school had been struggling for years and with the rapid expansion of the town over the course of the Nineteenth Century the old Guildhall had long since been deemed unfit for purpose.

Top left: *Workhouse*. Top right: *Inside the workhouse*. Bottom right: *Entrance to the Grammar School.*

'In 1800 when the 'Old Guildhall' was taken down private interest prevailed powerfully to induce its re-erection on the same site, and in an evil hour, a man called Eveleigh, who had been Clerk of Works to some architect at Bath, undertook in so limited a space to provide room for a Guildhall, all the purposes of a Mayoralty House, as far as regards kitchens and their appendages and dining rooms; prisons for debtors as well as thieves, rogues and vagabonds, a newsroom, and withal a Market-place; such a preposterous plan could only be approved by ignorant men who unfortunately at this time governed the affairs of the Corporation; it met with very general reprehension and some feeble opposition amongst the inhabitants, but nothing effectual was done to impede its progress. And thus £7,000 was spent in erecting a structure, which soon was found to be inadequate for the purposes of a prison, but moderately adapted to the purposes of a Guildhall, and totally inefficient as a place for a hall of justice ... so much for our modern improvements.' The building was 'condemned almost from the first' (Wright) as being 'inconvenient and unworthy, in every respect, of the important town to which it belongs.' (Worth)

Thus it was that the Corporation determined to erect a new and altogether bigger complex and when the new Guildhall was opened in 1874, this building lay empty until September 1876 when the newly established Plymouth Free Library was opened here. The new usage quickly proved successful and in its first two years there were almost 250,000 book issues recorded, an impressive statistic as there were only about 10,000 books in the library. The news rooms were also busy. Here many daily and weekly journals were on stands, with monthlies and quarterlies on the tables. 'These rooms,' noted the in-house librarian William Wright, 'are very popular and thronged at all hours of the day.'

Top: *Eveleigh's 'unworthy' Guildhall at the junction of Whimple Street and, beyond, Looe Street and High Street.*
Above left: *Looking east along Whimple Street.* Above right: *Inside the cramped council chamber.*

Just along from the Free Library, on the corner of Whimple Street and Kinterbury Street we find the oldest bank in Plymouth, the Naval Bank, currently styled Messrs Harris, Bulteel & Co., in the hands of the present partners Thomas Bulteel, JP, of Radford House, Plymstock and Mr Percy F Bulteel, of the Retreat, Plymstock, who is also Treasurer of the Plymouth Chamber of Commerce.

There are twelve Branches and Agencies of the Naval Bank. Meanwhile, further down Kinterbury Street, currently occupying Nos. 4, 5 and 6 is Micklewood's the wholesale manufacturing stationer. Until recently incidentally, the site of No.6 was occupied by one of the most ancient houses in the borough — it was demolished in 1891.

Top left: *Looking south down Kinterbury Street towards Whimple Street, with the Naval Bank (top right) on the corner.*
Above left and right: *Micklewood's print factory.* Inset: *An early Co-op shop in Kinterbury Street.*

PLYMOUTH: A MODERN TOWN

As already noted, the Georgian Guildhall, built on the site of its Jacobean predecessor at the junction of High Street and Whimple Street, was never really deemed to have met the criteria for which it was designed. It was, it was claimed, 'inconvenient as a guildhall, unsuited for a mayoralty house, totally inadequate as a prison, and perfectly absurd for market purposes'.

'Plymothians', wrote Worth in 1890, 'were not long content with this multum in parvo' [too much too little] and less than thirty years after its completion were looking to build something bigger and better. 'But threatened men live on' continued Worth, 'and so Eveleigh's ugly building long continued at the centre of civic life in Plymouth.'

It wasn't until the new workhouse was erected at Greenbank in 1858 that it was decided that the most central site for a new Guildhall would be west of St Andrew's Church. This was where the old workhouse stood, at the top of Catherine Street.

Over the next ten years the Corporation systematically bought up neighbouring properties, the Orphan's Aid Charity buildings and adjoining lands and houses in Basket Street and Westwell Street. Westwell Street itself, as one of the main approaches to this site, was widened at the same time. Not everyone was in favour of the grand scheme going ahead but when, in 1869, a meeting was called 'unavailingly' in opposition to the project, it was decided to invite plans from architects and to offer three prizes for the best.

In all 20 sets of designs were submitted and, having called in a professional architect, Mr Waterhouse, the Council chose the designs of the Plymouth-based firm of Messrs Alfred Norman and James Hine. The next step was to invite tenders for the execution of the work and, in the early part of 1870, twelve were submitted, the Council finding in favour of that sent in by Messrs Call & Pethick. The original quote was for £32,475. Pethick carried out the work and as is so often the case, the eventual bill was considerably more than was anticipated. The final cost was about half as much again, almost £50,000.

On Thursday 28 July at precisely 2.30pm the Mayor and Corporation met outside the old Guildhall and walked 'thence in Procession to the spot' where the foundation stone for the new Guildhall was to be laid. At three o'clock, they had met up with the contractors, architects and architect's clerks, bearing implements; the town surveyor, corporate officers, councillors, aldermen, magistrates, police and town sergeants bearing maces and the Vicar of St Andrew's, Charles Wilkinson, who offered up prayer. Then the Chairman of the Guildhall Committee, Alfred Rooker, invited the Mayor, William Luscombe, 'to lay the stone.' After that, the Mayor was given a silver trowel by the architects and, once the formalities had been concluded, the various dignitaries retired to the Royal Hotel for a Public Commemorative Dinner.

Four years later, on the morning of Thursday 13 August 1874, an even grander occasion marked the official opening of the completed buildings. Officiating this time was the Prince of Wales, Queen Victoria's eldest son Albert Edward, Lord High Steward of the Borough of Plymouth and the future Edward VII, then aged 33. Alfred Rooker was now enjoying his second term as Mayor (he had earlier held office in 1851) and this time the celebrations lasted not one, but three days.

This page: 28 July 1870, the foundation stone is laid for the new Guildhall.
Opposite page: 13 August 1874 the opening ceremony.

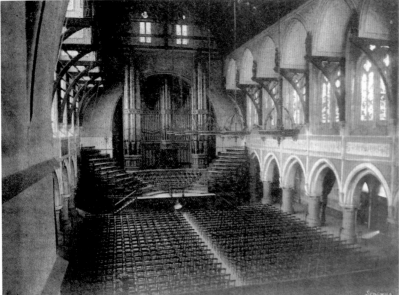

As the assembled crowds waited for the Prince to be handed the silver key, trumpeters played a Grand Festival March specially written for the occasion by the 30-year-old organist of Sherwell Church, Frederick Lohr. After the formal opening there was a 'Dejeuner in the Great Hall' of the new building and then in the evening there were 'Illuminations and Fireworks'. Over the next two days a Grand Musical Festival was held, the principal works performed being, on the Friday, Mendelssohn's Elijah, and on the Saturday evening at 7pm, Haydn's Creation. A Grand Rehearsal for Inmates of the Charitable Institutions was held earlier on the Saturday. A truly grand spectacle it must have been too with a mixed choir of almost 300 and a band containing over 80 musicians.

The opening of the Guildhall was later to be the subject of one of the 14 great stained-glass windows that ran down the sides of the Great Hall, while another depicted the reception held here the following day when the Freemasons of Devon and Cornwall met here and welcomed the Prince of Wales as their Grand Master.

The Great hall itself is 'capable of seating 3,000 persons, with an orchestra, and at one end, a gallery capable of holding 260 persons; several small ante-rooms are attached, and there are no less than seven doors to the hall, thereby ensuring perfect facility of ingress and egress.

'All the principal concerts take place in this hall, in which there is a fine organ, and a promenade concert is given every Saturday night, at which one or more of the military bands generally play.

There are also Sessions and Police Courts, Magistrates' rooms and all necessary offices, whilst in the rear are the Police Station and drill yard.

Top: *The opening Dejeuner in the Great Hall 13 August 1874.* Bottom: *The Guildhall laid out for a concert.*
Right: *One of Fouracre's 14 windows for the Great Hall, this one depicting a scene from the Civil War.*

Looking east from Westwell Street, across the Guildhall Square to St Andrew's Church.

Atop the various gable ends of the new complex of buildings are a number of eminent sculptures with Drake depicted at the apex of the Council Chamber. Inside the Great Hall there are more — of British monarchs, including Queen Victoria. At ground level there is one further piece, of Alfred Rooker, a leading local solicitor who had been Mayor in 1851-52, and was appointed Chairman of the Guildhall Committee in the lead up to and execution of the building of Plymouth's Victorian Guildhall and Municipal Building complex.

It was no great surprise therefore that this most prominent of Plymouth's leading citizens (he only narrowly missed out on being elected MP in 1871) was invited to be Mayor a second time so that he could officiate at the opening of the new civic development in August 1874. At the end of this second session in the Mayoral seat the 60-year-old Rooker decided to take his wife, Elizabeth, and their two daughters, Alice and Mary (both in their 20s) away from their home in Hartley Road on a trip to the Holy Land.

Sadly for the eminent solicitor — who had never known a day's illness — he was struck by fever journeying between Damascus and Baalbeck in Lebanon. With modes of medical care and transport limited he was carried by eight men in a litter before picking up a horse-drawn carriage to take him onto Beirut were he was seen, first by an English doctor and then an American physician. Sadly, however, they were unable to help and on the fifth day into his fever Rooker died. Not long after the news reached Plymouth a public subscription was set up to raise funds for a statue to the much respected man and some £1,500 was raised.

Top and middle: 20 September 1878 - Rooker's statue unveiled outside the new Municipal Building. Bottom: The statue in context.

Alfred Rooker

In executing his work the sculptor Stephens depicted Rooker in Mayoral robes with a plan of the Guildhall in hand. The official unveiling took place on 20 September 1878 and among those we see in this photograph are William Square, local surgeon and acquaintance of Rooker who read a tribute to his friend, and Joseph Wills the then current Mayor.

The unveiling of Rooker's memorial had, as a partial backdrop to the proceedings, St Andrew's Church Hall.

Erected in the 1870s, the Hall enjoyed but a brief existence. It stood on the site of the Georgian vicarage attached to St Andrew's and was removed shortly after the death of the long-serving John Hatchard.

Used for a time as a skating-rink, the hall had been designed by JH Keats. However, it wasn't long before increasing pressure on the town's first purpose-built Post Office on the corner of St Andrew Street and Whimple Street saw the hall pulled down and a brand new Post Office erected in its stead. Opened just a couple of weeks before Christmas 1884, the new facility was designed by EG Rivers, Chief Engineer of the HM Office of Works, who was responsible for many other public buildings around the country.

The Postal Service saw massive expansion across the country during this period, much of it in the wake of the introduction of the postage stamp in 1840.

That same year, Treville Street witnessed the birth of Edward Stanley Gibbons, who, after a brief spell as a clerk with the Naval Bank, entered his father's pharmacy business in Treville Street.

Before long, young Gibbons had persuaded his father to allow him to indulge his passion for buying and selling stamps in a corner of the pharmacy and by 1862 he was doing more business than his father.

In 1865 he produced a price list in the form of a magazine and created the world's first stamp catalogue.

In 1872 he moved to bigger premises in his own right and two years later he moved again, this time out of the town, to London.

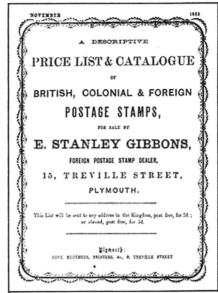

NOVEMBER 1865

A DESCRIPTIVE

PRICE LIST & CATALOGUE

OF

BRITISH, COLONIAL & FOREIGN

POSTAGE STAMPS,

FOR SALE BY

E. STANLEY GIBBONS,

FOREIGN POSTAGE STAMP DEALER,

15, TREVILLE STREET,

PLYMOUTH.

This List will be sent to any address in the Kingdom, post free, for 2d.; or abroad, post free, for 3d.

Plymouth:
COVE BROTHERS, PRINTERS, &c., 9, TREVILLE STREET

Above left and right: Stanley Gibbons and his pioneering stamp catalogue. Left: Penny Black. Right: Three angles on the same Westwell Street site. Top: St Andrew's vicarage 870. Middle: St Andrew's Hall 1883 Bottom: Plymouth's new Post Office opened in 1884.

The old St Andrew's burial yard that sat on the northern side of the mother church.

As mentioned, Plymouth's first purpose-built Post Office was at the top of St Andrew Street on the corner of Whimple Street, a site that, oddly enough, had been home to an even earlier incarnation of the St Andrew's vicarage.

'It was erected in 1847-48 by a company of shareholders, at a cost of £3,000, from designs furnished by Oswald Arthur, Esq., after the style of the temple of Vesta, at Tivoli, Italy — presenting two fronts, comprising an arcade supporting ten Corinthian pilasters and entablature, surmounted with a light ornamental balustrade.

'The windows are ornamented with enriched trusses, from which are suspended wreaths of fruit and foliage; and the royal arms is introduced in the angular front. The whole of the business is transacted on the ground floor, the upper rooms being the postmaster's private apartments.' (SHtoPDS 1851)

The first Post Master to take up residency here was Charles Markes, who had been appointed in 1833. From his upper floors he had a fine view across the top of St Andrew's burial yard. From the ground floor his outlook, and that of his customers, looking to the west was dominated by the said graveyard, rising up from ground level to well above head height.

But however great an inconvenience that was deemed to be by the pedestrians it was an even greater impediment to any form of wheeled transport.

Coach and carriage operators had a tight turn coming out of Old Town Street and into Bedford Street and these, after all, are two of the main commercial thoroughfares in the town. Add trams into the mix and you have an even greater problem.

Thus it was that in 1884 the ground was levelled and the remains were reverently removed to the Westwell Street burial ground.

Finally cleared of all obstructions, in 1893 the Diocese consented to transfer the ownership of the now open site on the north side of the church to the Mayor of Plymouth — part of it 'for no other purpose than the enjoyment of the public ... to be enclosed with railings'.

Above: The narrow lane running down to St Andrew's tower and much below it was cleared in the 1860s to make way for the new Guildhall and Municipal Building complex. Right top: Basket Street too was cleared in all but name. Middle and bottom: The new Basket Street looking west and east.

On Tuesday 30 May 1895 a large crowd assembled to witness the transfer of the conveyance, the opening of the area, and the inauguration of James Hine's distinctive cross.

Made up of alternate layers of red sandstone and the typically creamy Portland stone, in each of the four faces of the pedestal, or bottom tier, within a moulded arch was placed a slab of polished granite.

The northern and southern slabs are respectively inscribed: 'The glory of God, and in memory of Parishioners during many centuries buried near this cross. I am the resurrection and the life,' and 'Erected Anno Domini 1894, Ven Archdeacon Wilkinson, John P Paige, T Greek Wills, Churchwardens'.

Within a recess on each face of the second tier is a statue. On the north, facing Bedford Street, is Peace, wearing a crown; on the east looking down Whimple Street is Faith, with a cross; on the south, facing the church, is Hope with an anchor; while on the west overlooking the Municipal Building is Charity, with an orphaned child.

Meanwhile, on one of the gateways of the enclosed railings, (erected at the expense of the town) is the inscription:

Top: The view from the old Post Office, with the burial yard. Bottom: The same view without the churchyard.

Left: St Andrew's Cross looking north east. Right: Looking west.

'Opened 30 May, 1895, Law, Mayor, E Rosevear, Chairman, Hoe and Park Committee.'

The cross itself stands as a Memorial to the 40 bodies that were disinterred for reburial at the Westwell site, and the many others that were left undisturbed.

The opening up of this busy part of town brought space and light to every angle and its impact was immediate. Certainly it had the effect of rendering the Bedford Hotel one of the more conspicuous landmarks in the area, it also greatly improved the views from many of the rooms.

Of course the introduction of steam and horse trams the previous decade had added considerably to the congestion on what were already the town's busiest streets. Competition for the roads from other horse traffic meant that accurate time-keeping was difficult and, after complaints from the public became ever more voluminous, the Corporation were eventually prompted to take action.

In 1892 they paid £12,500 for the Plymouth Tramways Company's fleet of red-and-cream liveried vehicles and Plymouth Corporation Tramways Department was formed. CR Everson was appointed General Manager, and among his many challenges was how to keep up the pressure for widening and improving roads.

Looking down Guildhall Square, Basket Street and Bedford Street.

Top: 1860s — the churchyard extending right into Bedford Street and the southern side of Basket Street still in place. Bottom: Same view, post-1895.

Of course it wasn't just the tram routes that were affected by the increasing amounts of traffic on the streets. Bedford Street, one of the main commercial arteries of the town, was finding itself increasingly unsuited to the modern world.

In the golden age of the coaching era the Globe Hotel had been one of the town's premier inns. It had been on the western edge of town and very near Frankfort Gate, indeed Bedford Street was then known as Frankfort Lane. However, the gate had come down in 1783 and the neighbouring street and avenues had been widened and improved for the first time.

Now it was time to look at the street again, the hotel was no longer a prime target for travellers, the arrival of the Iron Horse — the railway — had changed all that, the best hotel locations now were within easy reach of a railway station.

Furthermore, although it had been greatly extended at the beginning of the Nineteenth Century, it had been eclipsed in size by many of the institutions that had arrived in the wake of the steam train and there were more commercial pressures coming to bear in the centre of town.

Just as the removal of the burial yard at St Andrew's had opened up new vistas at the eastern end of Bedford Street, so the demolition of the Globe Hotel, temporarily at least, created a number of intriguing new vantage points.

They weren't available for long, however, and soon the imposing neo-Gothic, red-brick Prudential Assurance Company building had risen high above the Globe's original footprint.

It is a move typical of many being made around the town centre as more and more ancient edifices were being pulled down to make way for taller structures offering two or three times the amount of floorspace of the buildings they were replacing. In many instances they are set back a little from the original street line to provide a wider thoroughfare but seldom at the expense of creating more commercial opportunities.

Opposite page and this page: clockwise from top left: The Globe Hotel, exterior; interior; the Globe's Frankfort Street elevation viewed from bottom of Cornwall Street and then same view without Globe and Kerswill's looking across to the eastern end of George Street; Bedford Street with the Prudential building; final view looking over the site of the Globe towards the western end of Bedford Street and the entrance to Frankfort Street; Bedford Street narrows; the east end of Bedford Street and Spooners; and a earlier wider view of Bedford Street and the Globe.

Top: *Bedford Street late-1870s with the Island.* Bottom: *The 'Island' has gone. The Borough Arms is second from the left and the Devon & Cornwall Bank just beyond it (on the far left in the top picture).*

Writing in 1879, Wright describes Bedford Street as the Fleet Street of Plymouth, 'for here again the business establishments are many and important.' Then he added: 'One drawback exists in the narrowness of a portion of the thoroughfare, but this will shortly be removed by the demolition of the block of buildings known as "The Island".'

Among the many commercial premises here were those of VJ Vickery & Co. and Underwood & Co. both of whom would subsequently relocate to other properties in Bedford Street and both of whom, later still, would merge with a business that was established in Bedford Street in the 1880s — that of Edward Dingle & Co. general draper and silk merchant.

Meanwhile, to return to Wright as our guide once more, he pauses here for a moment, 'to take a survey of the newly opened coffee house — the Borough Arms — the first fruits of the establishment of the Plymouth Coffee House Company. 'This establishment was opened in October 1878, and is intended to supply a want in our social system and as an inducement to sobriety. The house was formerly in the occupation of Messrs. Radford & Son, and known as London House. It is now well, and in some respects, elegantly fitted; having refreshment-bars on each floor, provided with urns for the supply of tea, coffee, and cocoa, besides solids of various kinds. The decorations are of a very attractive character. Handsome white marble tables and comfortable chairs form the furniture of each room while newspaper stands, to accommodate the London and local daily papers, are provided in the downstairs bar. On the ground floor is a spacious saloon where meetings are held, and once during the week a popular entertainment provided.

30, BEDFORD ST., PLYMOUTH. 30,

E. DINGLE

GENERAL

DRAPER

AND **LADIES' OUTFITTER,**

INVITES INSPECTION TO HIS STOCK OF

**Black Silks and Velvets,
Dress Materials,
Mantles and Jackets,
Millinery,
Costumes and Skirts.**

BABY-LINEN & LADIES' UNDERCLOTHING.

DRESS-MAKING, MANTLE-MAKING, & MILLINERY

ORDERS EXECUTED ON THE PREMISES.

Under experienced Management, at the shortest notice.

Every Requisite for FAMILY MOURNING in Stock.

'Attached to the upstairs bar are private rooms for ladies; and on the upper floor, club-rooms, the board-room and other conveniences.

'On the other side of Bank Street is the Devon and Cornwall Bank, a substantial building, with granite front. This is the headquarters of the Devon and Cornwall Banking Company, Alfred Hingston, Esq. JP being the resident Manager.'

'Bank Street is the new home of the Young Men's Christian Association, recently revived, and now numbering 200 members. The objects of the association are to provide "Social comfort, intellectual culture, physical development, and spiritual help for young men." Phonetic, Microscopic, Elocutionary and other classes are held, as well as Bible and Devotional classes on Sundays and throughout the week.' (Wright 1879)

In 1887 the YMCA moved again, this time to a purpose-built headquarters on the other side of Bedford Street, on the corner of Westwell Street.

Two doors down from that junction, at No.16½ Bedford Street, above the Three Towns Dairy, we found the home of Coupe and Bennett, Photographers.

'It is a noteworthy fact that there is no art which has made a more rapid progress during recent years than that of photography. Whereas but a few years ago, people were obliged to wear a pleasing countenance for some minutes in order that they might be transferred to card-boards with an amiable expression, they may now be photographed instantaneously, and every line of character is brought out forcibly.

'The different effects of light and shade are manifest in the more recent pictures, which have become veritable works of art.

'In this connection we make mention of Coupe & Bennett's photographic establishment. On the top floor will be found one of the finest studios in the West of England, replete with all the latest novelties in backgrounds and accessories, apparatus and appliances.' (Wright 1894)

Top left: Devon & Cornwall Bank. Top right: Coupe & Bennett's studio. Above: Two military outfitters from Bedford Street: Walling and Pearse & Son.

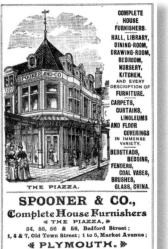

Bedford Street houses a wide variety of business premises, it was also home to the second highest concentration of linen drapers in the town.

The greatest number, around the middle of the century, were to be found in Whimple Street (which had acquired its name from the great number of hood or hat sellers based there). In the 1830s Joseph Spooner — silk mercer, draper and straw bonnet manufacturer — started up his business there and by the 1860s he had opened additional premises in Bedford Street.

The move went well and Spooner, realising there was a demand for diversification, opened a carpet and a furnishing department in Old Town Street. It was around the same time that a former Spooner's manager Edward Dingle left to set up his own business.

As the 1890s dawned Spooner & Co. adopted a new logo or trademark — a ship's wheel inscribed with their name and address, or at least core address, as the enterprise now has half a dozen or so addresses — in Bedford Street, the Piazza and Old Town Street.

The impression of a number of shops all dotted around the town centre is, however, a misleading one, as for the most part, these properties are all interconnected, forming in essence one large block, Spooner's Corner, overlooking St Andrew's Cross.

At the beginning of the 1890s Old Town Street itself gave every indication of what its name implied, that it was one of the oldest streets in the town. But all that was about to change and by the end of the decade it is now more truly be described as one of the most modern streets in Plymouth.

Top left: *The corner of Bedford Street and Old Town Street, not yet Spooner's Corner as the building depicted here, in a nod to modernity, is known as the Telegraph Inn (it had been known as the Jubilee). Right and above: Spooner's advertising, the colour ad showing both the Piazza building (in the smaller ad) and Spooner's Corner (to the left of St Andrew's Cross).*

Opposite: *Old Town Street c18*

'There was living in Old Town Street, not more I believe than 20 years ago, an extremely old lady, who kept a tripe shop there, and who remembered the time — probably about when Dr Johnson was here — when most of the houses in Old Town Street were covered with thatch. Could this venerable individual be permitted to revisit the scene of her mortal occupation, and supposing she had a taste for architecture as well as tripe, she would be rather interested, as well as astonished, I think, in noticing in the place of her old shop and other old buildings, (which if they had no other recommendation were at least easy to get at when the roofs and chimney tops were out of order) an assemblage of great houses in the Roman-Corinthian, Anglo-Italian, Lombardo-Venetian, and other styles too numerous to mention, constituting a sort of second edition in bricks and mortar of Mr Wightwick's "Palace of Architecture".'
(James Hine 1861)

When 31-year-old Hine was writing, the street line of Old Town Street still had the curves the old lady would have recognised but, apart perhaps for one or two ancient inns, the properties lining the street had doubtless changed quite significantly; however, what our architect friend, Mr Hine, could not have known then was just how much Old Town Street would change within his lifetime over the next 40 years.

Opposite page: *Looking down Old Town Street towards the Old Four Castles, curving around in front of what was then one of the street's newer buildings, Stidston's drapers, is Old Town Avenue.* Top left: *The Old Four Castles and the bottom end of Old Town Street.* Top right: *Stidston's is in the distance, we're curving around to the top of Old Town Street (above) to meet Tavistock Road and Tavistock Place and St Luke's Chapel.*

One of the great many changes he witnessed was the demolition of the ancient Noah's Ark. Although technically in Saltash Street, the Noah's Ark was next door to Edward Jasper's delightfully slate-hung tailor's shop which had an Old Town Street address.

The common link between the photographs that appear on these two pages, Jasper's stood on the corner of Drake Street, thus in some respects it was somehow appropriate that when the Noah's Ark was rebuilt it should have been in a Victorian mock-Elizabethan style.

Drake Street is a small but busy side street and is one of a number of routes into the Market at the back of Old Town Street, while Saltash Street leads up to the Ebenezer Chapel.

Meanwhile, continuing our journey along Old Town Street, we pass another slate-hung property, the Bedford Wine and Spirit Vaults. This charming edifice is destined to be one of only two of the old Old Town Street hostelries to survive the 1890s (Golden Lion was the other). It stands on the corner of a very small and narrow cut in, Caxton Mews, leading to the stables with a side entrance to the Wine & Spirit Vaults.

As we see here the tram route originally ran through this stretch, making the Vaults' wall a popular location for advertisers. But that has changed as the area once known as Old Town Without, just beyond the Old Town Gate, has been sidelined again.

Left: *Three views of the much altered Noah's Ark shortly before its demolition and replacement with the triple gabled building we see in the photograph above.*

A horse tram swings around the top of Old Town Street, about to pass in front of the Bedford Wine and Spirit Vaults.

In the early days of the tram service, trams didn't run down the length of Old Town Street. Most routes in Plymouth itself ran out of Russell Street, but there was one that ran north from Market Avenue and the panier market, a popular 'community centre'. This service went through the top end of Old Town Street and was a horse-drawn system. Plymouth also experimented with steam-pulled tram cars. However, as electricity made an increasingly large impact on the town the prospect of the electrification of the tram system became plausible, but the lower part of Old Town Street was too narrow to entertain such an idea, unless of course, there was some way of widening the busy thoroughfare.

Thus it came to pass that centuries of history were swept away in the name of progress. Among the most conspicuous casualties were two venerable inns, the Old Four Castles and the Rose and Crown. Both were believed to be well over 300 years old and although little is known about either, the landlord of the Old Four Castles, Thomas Pike, struck a special token in 1657 when Cromwell was declared 'Lord Protector of the Commonwealth'.

The former was named after the erstwhile medieval fortification on Lambhay Hill that was superseded by Drake's fort in the 1590s, while the latter is considered, nominally if not literally, to be a throwback to the fifteenth century War of the Roses.

Both pubs sat on the east side of Old Town Street and were among dozens of properties to be demolished in the 1890s — although, at least in the case of the Rose and Crown, which stood on the corner of Week Street, a new, much taller edifice, bearing the same name, has been built on the same site.

Above: Best's Old Four Castles c1890 Middle: 1890 advertisement for Four Castles Tea. Right: Dilleigh's Tea Warehouse, 1894, standing opposite the Old Four Castles and destined to survive.

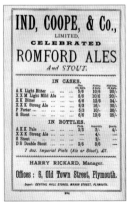

Top left: *The Rose and Crown, Old Town Street.* Bottom left: *The Rose and Crown with a view down Week Street c1980.* Top right: *The new Rose and Crown.* Above left: *Ind Coope ad.* Middle: *A doomed slate-hung property in Old Town Street.* Right: *Smith & Co. mantle sellers, and survivors in Old Town Street.*

Doidge's Western Counties Illustrated Annual. 37

WILLIAM H. LAKE,
Tailor and Breeches Maker.

Newest Designs in Shooting, Fishing and Cycling Suits.

Specialité: BREECHES MAKING. Fit and Style Guaranteed.

LIVERIES, UNIFORMS, &c. · HOSIERY.
· · · SHIRTS MADE TO ORDER. · · ·

EBRINGTON HOUSE,
2, EBRINGTON ST, PLYMOUTH.

Week Street and Treville Street emerged from the reconstruction exercise largely unscathed. But, we cannot say the same for Ebrington Street as this thoroughfare also found itself on the proposed new tram route. In order to effect such proposals the entire western end of the street was removed. The works were executed throughout the 1890s and the process began with the closing down of buildings prior to demolition. At the beginning of the decade the entrance to Ebrington Street was some 50 yards to the west of its current location as evidenced here by the photograph of the old Ebrington House on the corner of Old Town Street, and then the new Ebrington House on the corner of Garden Street.

Previously, Alfred Geach had been running a Tailors, Hatters, and Outfitters business from here, but he relocated to Treville Street and when the new building of the same name opened it was William Lake, Tailor and Breeches Maker, who moved in.

The displacement involved is apparent in the photograph on the opposite page in which we see the earlier street-line of Old Town Street in the foreground, by the horse and dust cart and the new Ebrington House in the middle distance above the horse.

Top left: *The original Ebrington House at the entrance to Ebrington Street.* Top right: *An advertisement for William Lake, the proprietor of the new Ebrington House.* Above left: *Looking up Garden Street towards Park Street.* Above right: *Looking down Garden Street to Ebrington Street with the Unity public house on the corner.*

Standing in Old Town Street, looking across the scene of much demolition to the new Ebrington House on what is the new western end of Ebrington Street. Inset far left: Another view from the top of Garden Street. Near left: Looking eastwards past soon-to-be-demolished part of Ebrington Street.

One of the determining elements in the decision to remove the eastern side of Old Town Street is that in comparatively recent times quite large sections of the western site have already been redeveloped as typified by the block now occupied by Stidstons who have now been in the street for more than 20 years.

From the map shown below it will become apparent just how dramatic the changes have been to this street, the main north route out of the town. The new tram lines have been laid along what was formerly the line of the shop fronts on the eastern side and thus this section has doubled in width, as indeed has Ebrington Street where it was the north side of the thoroughfare that was sacrificed.

It will also be noted that Garden Street has disappeared and an entirely new and much wider route driven through that site. The western end of Park Street has also been flattened and assimilated into Old Town Street as far as Duke Street or Spear's Corner, as it is known.

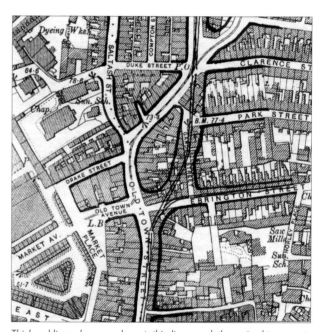

Top: c1895, a horse tram exits Old Town Avenue, turning north into Old Town Street. Across the way we see that Ebrington House has just been demolished. Above: An electric tram enters a part of Ebrington Street that is soon to disappear, note the Plymouth Corporation Tramway offices on the left.

Thick red lines show new layout, thin lines mark the revised tram route.

Above: *Stidston's on the corner of Old Town Avenue.* Left: *The section here, jutting out into the street is about to disappear.* Right: *With Stidston's on the far right we're looking across to what was about to become a very rounded entrance into Ebrington Street, and the buildings shown left have gone.*

The first electricity cables in Plymouth are laid in Old Town Street, Ebrington Street and Ham Street. The authorities taking advantage of the street widening works.

Not everyone welcomed the imminent arrival of the electric tram. Some shopkeepers felt that it would make it difficult for some of their customers to leave their carriages outside their shops. Others, like James Taylor whose drapery business was on the west side of Old Town Street, on the corner of Old Town Avenue, only saw advantage in the situation, as even before the route was traction-driven by electricity he was keen to point out that: 'the terminus of the recent new line of tramcars is within one minute's walk of the shop, which will be a boon to visitors from Mutley, Mannamead, and the surrounding districts.'

Of course, the electrification of the tram route brought with it the beguiling potential for electric lighting in shops as well, but Plymouth has not exactly been quick to adopt the new invention.

The first public display of an electric light was back in April 1849, when Jonathan Hearder, at the invitation of the President of the Devonport Mechanics Institute, installed an arc lamp at the top of Devonport Column.

However, it wasn't until 1884, as we have seen, that there was any public use of the electric light, on Plymouth Pier. Four years later, electric lights were installed throughout the Theatre Royal, with a consequent reduction in their fire insurance, and in 1891 it was introduced into Devonport Dockyard.

Plymouth appointed its first Borough Electrical Engineer in 1898. The foundation stone for the Generating Station was laid in April of that year and the first cables appeared in the streets that were being redeveloped here — Old Town Street, Ebrington and Ham Street.

Lampposts for carrying power cables for the new traction trams are erected in Old Town Street

By the time the dust finally settled in and around Old Town Street the area became something of a magnet for photographers and postcard producers. In terms of the architecture, the retail offer, the tram service and the electric lighting, this was not only the most modern street in Plymouth, but possibly the whole of the South West.

Tall redbrick buildings lined the great wide boulevard, designed to accommodate pedestrians and the very latest forms of transport. Small wonder that rather than just leave them in monochrome the postcard manufacturers have been keen to take advantage of the latest technology available to them and produce hand-tinted, life-like versions of these vistas.

The main focal point for all of these new developments became a large lozenge-shaped block sitting in the fork now at the top of Old Town Street, a block henceforth known as Drake Circus. To the east, Ebrington Street and snaking around to the north was a new stretch of Old Town Street.

Top left: *Looking down the reconstructed Ebrington Street.* Top right: *Looking south down Old Town Street to Whimple Street.*
Above: *The new Drake Circus development with a new section of Old Town Street snaking around and north to Spear's Corner.*

The new taller, wider, state of the art Old Town Street.

Here, as we start to head north again and Old Town Street merges into Tavistock Road, we see all new developments on both sides of the road, while in the other images on these pages we see those structures that were forced to give way to the new arrangements.

Jethro Ham, the surgical bootmaker (his name, JN Ham, and number, 42 — his temporary address in Clarence Street — is clear for all to see, even from a distance), subsequently relocated to Tavistock Road. Tavistock Place was the address of the next-door property to Jethro's store and Spear's Corner (named after William Spear's drapery business at the end of Park Street) overlooking these two properties on the left. The Revenue Hotel on the right, is where we see a crowd congregated around the lamp-post in the middle of the photograph on the opposite page.

The buildings on the right at the end of Duke Street, were destined to survive, while everything we see on the left of that image and to the middle and left of the image in the bottom left-hand corner of this page, were due to be demolished.

If we were to go back in time and stand facing the other way we would have seen Samuel Ward's doomed jewellery shop, his clock being one of the reason's that Spear's Corner was such a popular meeting place.

Top: *The top of the refashioned Old Town Street leading into Tavistock Road. Above left: Looking down Tavistock Place to Spear's Corner, Samuel Ward's jewellery business is the last building in the terrace on the left and the first building we see looking north from Spear's Corner. Note the tramlines as they then ran down from Tavistock Place. Above right: Ward's conspicuous clock overlooking Spear's Corner.*

Above: *Spear's Corner looking down what was then still Tavistock Place, note the soon to be redundant tramlines in relatively new sets. Right: The view from St Luke's Chapel down a slightly more northerly section of those tramlines. The Revenue can just be seen in the distance, Regent Street is running off to the left. Although the street line was preserved here, the buildings weren't.*

A little further north we find our belated memorial to the Queen's Golden Jubilee.

'Early in the year 1887, the Mayor (Mr WH Alger) convened a public meeting to consider in what way the jubilee of her Majesty the Queen should be celebrated.

'A series of meetings followed to consider various proposals. Amongst others a statue of HM the Queen, a people's palace of delight, an art gallery, the restitution of the Citadel ground to the borough, that Drake Place Mills be adapted as a recreation ground, and the paying-off of the debt on the South Devon and East Cornwall Hospital.

'On 4 April the following resolutions were adopted: That the local jubilee memorial take the form of raising a fund for the establishment of a science and art school, in co-operation with the Town Council and with a view to the promotion of technical education.

'That the Town Council be requested to establish a science and art school in the borough, under the Free Library Act, and to grant a site for the purpose on the understanding that the funds for the erection of the necessary buildings be provided by voluntary contributions.' (WMN 8 October 1892)

As it transpired it was a little over five years later before the building was finished. Designed by Plymouth architect AD Shortridge and built by local contractor Alfred Debnam, the New Jubilee Science, Art and Technical Schools were erected on the site of the old cattle market and officially opened on Friday 7 October 1892.

Top: *The new Jubilee Science, Art and Technical School building opened in 1892, the Harvest Home lamp on the left.* Above: *Looking up the bottom end of Tavistock Road.* Right: *Further up Tavistock Road.*

Top left: *The corner of Glanville Street and Tavistock Road, just above the Technical School, the Butcher's Arms (a throwback to the cattle market days, on the corner.*
Top right: *The same stretch looking back down to the Harvest Home and the Technical Schools.* Above right: *The eastern side of Tavistock Road, a site earmarked for the new Museum and Art Gallery and Library — note part of the sign indicating to a Gentlemen's facility on the left.* Above left: *1888 ads for Tavistock Road businesses.*

Further up Tavistock Road the present century has seen even greater changes. Something of a rural hinterland when Victoria came to the throne, in 1825 and 1828 two reservoirs, drawing on Drake's Leat, had been erected here. In 1874 stonework from the old public conduit at the top of Old Town Street (demolished in 1834) was reconstructed in the wall, and in 1891 the two reservoirs were reconfigured as one. Just below, on the site originally of an old and derelict mill that was destroyed by fire in 1860, Sherwell Church was built, in September 1864, while on the other side of the road, Queen Anne Terrace was later erected on the former site of Sherwell House.

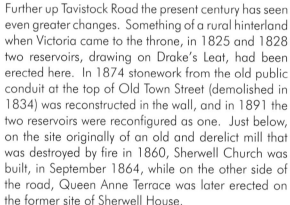

Clockwise from top left: Cole's Dartmoor Hotel (a reference no doubt to the water coming from the moor via Drake's Leat. The Hotel was demolished c1897 to celebrate the centenary of Norley Chapel (out of which Sherwell Church had grown). A second view of the Hotel. Sherwell Church with the hotel gone. Children on a tricycle above Sherwell Church. Sherwell House, demolished to make way for Queen Anne Terrace. Drake's Place Reservoir. The remnant of the conduit in the reservoir wall. Opposite page: Sherwell Church. Looking up North Hill and Tavistock Road. Bottom: A tracer — an additional horse — is required to take this Plymouth Corporation Tram up the hill.

The first tram route north out of the town to Mutley ran not along Tavistock Road but the somewhat less steep Houndiscombe Road, the route taken by Drake's Leat.

In 1895, however, after ten years had passed, a new route was opened along North Hill via Tavistock Place ... and later, after the improvements alluded to above, via Tavistock Road into Old Town Street. Prior to electrification this route clearly took its toll on the horse. Trace horses, for this section and for Townsend Hill, were stabled at Belgrave Mews. Between them the stables at Compton (the terminus), Mutley, and Millbay served some 250 horses.

A day's work for a tram horse is 10-12 hours, with a working life of five years before they are generally put down.

Before heading out further north let us venture back down Old Town Street and let Mr Wright take us 'through the Market gates, and find ourselves in an extensive enclosure, with little claim to good arrangement or appearance of effected buildings.'

The Market in fact, is large but inconvenient, and quite unworthy of so important a town.

'It is however probable that, ere long [he was writing in 1879] the Town Council, having overcome the burden of providing a new Townhall and Municipal Buildings; may face the next great question, namely, the need for the erection of a new market, on the present site, but with a fine street running through it, as a continuation of the street we have just left.

'Such a scheme has been mooted, and will, doubtless, soon be made a reality.

'The Market, which opened in 1804, occupies an area of three acres, and contains covered vegetable, butter, fish, and poultry markets, butchers' stalls, earthenware markets, besides shops and stalls for the sale of clothing and general merchandise.'

Fifteen years later it was possible to say 'Our Markets are excellent, and are well supplied with superior animal food, agricultural produce, fish, and, in fact, all the necessaries of life are to be obtained of the best quality at moderate prices, which is more than can be said of some of the watering places, where the charges for everything in this way are extravagant.' (Wright 1894)

M. H. GREEN,
Wholesale and Retail
DRIED FISH MERCHANT,
9, Market Avenue, Plymouth.

- - Smoked Sprats a speciality. - -
Smoked Salmon, Cod's Roes, Haddocks, &c.,
FINEST QUALITY!   LOWEST PRICES!

PLYMOUTH EGG & BUTTER STORE,
15, Arcade, Plymouth Market.

To Farmers: Best Prices given for Fresh Eggs and Butter.

Top: *Early view of the nineteenth-century market off East Street.*
Bottom: *Inside the extensive enclosure.* Right: *1898 Advertisement.*

The Market had, by this time, just received the much hoped for overhaul, the crowning glory of which was the new Corn Exchange — although not everyone was happy with the name: 'The Exchange should be a free market to all comers, as I believe every other market is in this country excepting the London Stock Exchange, or such places as are formed by corporate mercantile bodies for the furtherance of their own particular trades. In this instance a really splendid and costly chamber has been built at the expense of Plymouth ratepayers for the benefit of Plymothians in general, and not for the corn trade or any other trade in particular.

'There is no reason why in a great importing town such as this that it should be called the "Corn Exchange", because as a matter of fact large importers of nitrate, timber and coal, and the manufacturers of manures and agricultural implements, and other local makers and vendors, constantly resort to it in order to meet their town and country customers.' (W Cecil Wade WMN 1893)

Top: *1894 advertisement for Martin & Palmer's New Pharmacy in the rebuilt Plymouth Market.* Above: *The new Arcade.* Right: *The 1893 Corn Exchange.*

Another route leading off Old Town Street takes us through Saltash Street, at the top of which we find the Ebenezer Chapel of the Westley Methodists ... 'erected in 1817, at a cost of about £5,000. It has a burial ground (now disused), schoolrooms and preacher's houses attached, and has recently been very much improved and enlarged.' (Wright 1879)

With all the improvements taking place in and around Old Town Street in the 1890s it was perhaps inevitable that the Ebenezer Chapel should have been refurbished too.

'During a considerable portion of the past summer the congregation worshipping at the Ebenezer Wesleyan Chapel have had their place of assembly in the hands of the builder and the decorator.

'In the first place, commencing with the roof this has been entirely renewed, the old ceiling has been taken away, and a handsome new panelled one put in its place. Three fine brass pendants, each with 60 lights, have also been added, with good effect.

'The whole of the windows of the chapel, which were of plain glass, have been removed and replaced by handsome cathedral glass of chaste design by Mr Fouracre, of Chapel Street.

'The panelling of the gallery is in two shades of terracotta relieved with salmon and light green, and the effect of this harmonises thoroughly with the wall decoration, which is quiet and pleasing.

'The work of the gilding and painting has been ably carried out by Messrs Harris & Sons, of George Street. All the seats in the chapel have been thoroughly cleaned and varnished. What will be the most noticeable alteration in the chapel, however, is the conversion of the pulpit into a rostrum. This has been done by adding a wing on either side of the handsome old-fashioned mahogany pulpit. The same kind of wood has been used, and the rostrum is now one of the most imposing in the Three Towns.

'It is supported on fine pillars coloured with a woven shade of terracotta. The organ behind the pulpit also needed attention, and it was decided to spend about £350 over it, the work of renovation being entrusted to Mr John Hele, who had added new mechanism and stops. The lighting of the chapel generally has been thoroughly overhauled, and this work has been efficiently done by Mr H Lawry.

'A valuable addition has been made to the chapel in the shape of a room on the south side, which will be used for church meetings of various kinds. The whole of the alterations have been carried out by Mr T May, contractor, under the direction of Mr HJ Snell architect.

'The reopening service will commence at noon on Wednesday with a prayer meeting.

'There will be a public luncheon afterwards, and at three o'clock the Rev John Bond of London will preach a service. A tea and an organ recital by John Hele will follow and in the evening there will be a public meeting in the Chapel.' (WMN 3 October 1892)

Top: *Ebenezer Chapel exterior view.* Middle: *Interior view after the 1892 refurbishment.*
Bottom: *The Ebenezer School House, with a view down Mill Lane on the right.*

Leaving Saltash Street ... 'a turning to the left leads to the entrance gateway of the works of the British & Irish Sugar Refining Company in Mill Lane, established by Messrs Bryant & Burnell in 1838, and merged into a Limited Liability Company in 1856. The works cover a very extensive area and include that of the old Frankfort Barracks, and also a part of the gardens of Sir Francis Drake, whose residence in Saltash Street was immediately contiguous. 'The company has a large business, employs nearly 150 hands, and consumes about 120 tons of coal per week. The machinery and arrangements are of the most complete and admirable kind.

'Returning to Saltash Street we proceed to the Public Free School in Cobourg Street. The school, founded in 1809, is the next to largest institution of the kind in the kingdom, having on an average 1,600 daily scholars in attendance.' (Wright 1879)

Above: *Portland Villas.* Top right: *Cobourg Street — Public Free School is on the left in the middle distance.* Right: *Cobourg Street Free School*

For the academically minded 'the most important and the oldest established library in the town, is the Plymouth and Cottonian Library, the handsome front of which is a feature of Cornwall Street.

'The building was erected (principally through the exertions of Mr George Eastlake) in 1812, from the design of Mr Foulston, and in 1852 additional rooms and a new frontage were added from the designs of Messrs Wightwick & Damant, for the reception of the Cottonian Collection, presented to the Institution by the late Mr William Cotton, FSA.

'The Library is approached from a spacious entrance hall, from which access is also obtained to the new room and to the staircase leading to the Cottonian Room.

'The Library itself is a lofty quadrangular room, 33-feet-square: at each angle a massive hollow pier with pilaster, supporting an entablature and cornice, from which spring elegant segmental arches. The whole is surmounted by a vaulted dome; in the centre rises a circular lantern, the roof of which is supported on fluted columns and between these columns a passage is left.

'Concealed in one of the piers is a spiral staircase giving access to the gallery which runs round all four sides of the room and divides it into two nearly equal heights.' *(Wright 1879)*

Albert, The Prince Consort, and Plymouth Corporation each donated £50 to the original subscription list for the Cottonian extension which includes 'a fine collection of books, prints, drawings, paintings, and works of Art and Vertu,' and 'is chaste apartment with an enriched coved ceiling, surmounted by a decorative lantern.' *(ibid)*

Left: Wightwick's new exterior to the Plymouth and Cottonian Library. Above: Inside the Library.

The Plymouth and Cottonian was not, however, a free library, although initially every proprietor did at least have the privilege (among others) 'of nominating one Young Man to the Library, between the Age of Fifteen and Twenty One years as a Reader'. That is, they could look, but not borrow.

A far more equitable arrangement was to become available at the Free Library, run by WHK Wright, and at the Co-operative Library and Newsroom. The latter had started life above the Co-op butcher's shop in Cornwall Street and moved, in 1894, to far more impressive premises in the spectacular new Central Building of the Plymouth Mutual Co-operative and Industrial Society on the corner of Frankfort Street and Courtenay Street.

The new Co-operative headquarters was a massive leap of faith for the Society. Back in November 1881 their committee had sanctioned the purchase of Nos. 17 and 18 Frankfort Street at a combined cost of £3,600 — the biggest single investment the Society had made to date — but then after six more years of spectacular growth: 'after much cogitation, we determined on utilising the property by building thereon a mighty erection worthy of our wealth, to which end we directed Mr Snell, the Society's architect, to prepare full plans for new buildings.'

As John Webb, the Co-op's first historian, locally, further noted in 1892, the move reflected 'the mighty power in pence properly directed and judiciously applied ... Barely 30 years had passed,' he added, 'since our first outlay of between £2 and £3, and here we found ourselves contemplating the outlay of at least £30,000 in one great block only ...'

The *Western Daily Mercury* described the building as being superior to any other block of business premises in the Three Towns. Great were the celebrations surrounding the opening ceremony. All those working for the Co-op in the Three Towns were allowed to attend and at 1.30pm an impressive procession of rolling-stock assembled at Friary. In all there were almost 50 wheeled vehicles, 11 horse-drawn bread vans, 3 milk floats, 16 hand-pushed milk barrows, 3 grocery vans, 5 oil wagons and 8 coal wagons and a 500-strong contingent on foot. A truly impressive display.

Top left: *Souvenir Programme from 1894.* Top right: *Inside the packing department.*
Right: *The new Central Premises complete with a hall capable of accommodating 1,000 people.*

While the impressive new premises of the Co-operative Society has done much to amend the retail focus in the town, along with those developments in Old Town Street and Ebrington Street, George Street very much clings on to its reputation as the Regent Street of Plymouth.

Here we find all manner of quality shops and businesses, among them that of Snell & Co., a firm that 'now holds the premier position in its line of business in the West of England'. *(Wright 1894)*

Established in 1859 in Devonport, the firm bears a close resemblance to the history of Sublime Tobacco itself in the rise of and development of the trade in this country.

'Well up in the lists of first-class Cigar Importers in this country, the premises at 17 George Street, have from time to time been enlarged, and being centrally situated amidst the principal establishments of the town, with an excellent display of goods, cannot fail to attract attention.'

Another of the well-established concerns, indeed they can trace their roots back to 1770 when George Street was first laid out as a residential thoroughfare, is that of Harris & Sons, House Painters and Decorators, Carvers and Gilders 'who are well-known, locally and elsewhere, as extensive contractors. Their transactions in the town and district, and far away from the precincts of Plymouth, have been very large, and are not in any way confined to ordinary buildings, many being ornaments to their respective localities. Amongst this class we may mention the decorating of the Guildhall, and portions of the Municipal Buildings; St Andrew's Church, Schools, and Hall; the Catholic Cathedral, the Chapel of the Convent of Notre Dame, Sherwell Chapel, Batter Street Chapel, the Grand Hotel, Exeter Street Mission Hall, the Jewish Synagogue, the Institution for the Blind, the Female Orphan Asylum, &c.' *(ibid)*

Top left: *General view of George Street.* Middle: *Snell & Co., exterior, interior, 1888 advert for Dunham & Collingwood (previous occupants of 17 George Street, Harris & Sons.* Bottom left: *Western end of George Street from Derry's Clock.*

George Street was a largely residential development until John Foulston, in 1811, decided that it was the ideal spot for a Theatre and Hotel, if such a complex was going to be economically viable, as it would need to be accessible by residents of all three towns, not just Plymouth.

Although the decision was met with a fair degree of scepticism on the part of the Corporation who had awarded him the contract, the decision soon turned what had been the far west extremity of the town into a vibrant commercial hub, and Union Street, Foulston's newly laid-out approach to Plymouth from Stonehouse and Devonport, was equally successful. It would nevertheless take a little longer for the 1,300-seater theatre to become self-sufficient. At the time, the Theatre and Hotel complex was the grandest enterprise the town had ever seen and Mr Foulston swiftly found his services in great demand. Work on the Athenaeum, another of his projects, began in 1818, five years after the completion of the Theatre Royal.

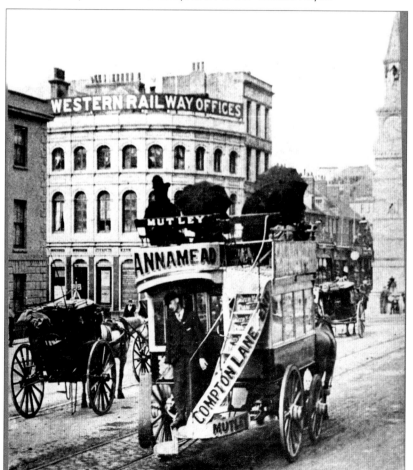

Top: *Royal Hotel, Theatre Royal, Athenaeum and Crescent Park with Derry's Clock, (Mayor Derry's wedding gift for the Prince of Wales and Princess Alexandra in 1862).* Middle: *View looking up Lockyer Street.* Bottom: *Looking further up Lockyer Street past St Andrew's Chapel of Ease and St Andrew's Terrace.* Far left: *A horse bus sets off from George Street for Compton Lane via Mutley.*

Top: *Horse tram in George Street waiting outside the Swan of Avon Hotel and the Office of the Western Morning News.* Bottom, left to right: *Inside and outside the offices.*

Another of those George Street businesses 'which rightly claims the distinction of being the leading concern in its own line of operation in Plymouth', is James Cousins' Hairdresser and Perfumer. 'As a competent and skilful perruquier, Mr Cousins supplies all kinds of wigs and head-dresses for whole or partial wear. His stock of the purest essences is one of the most comprehensive in Plymouth, besides which, a varied assortment of combs, brushes, washes, scented soaps, tooth brushes, etc., are kept with many other articles for decoration and use.' (Wright 1894)

Also based in George Street were the offices of the *Western Daily Mercury* and the *Western Morning News* — 'the leading daily paper of the West.' Launched on the same day as the local Co-operators made their initial investment in their Society, 3 January 1860, this has been a similar success story and in conjunction with the *Western Morning News* are issued the *Western Weekly News*, the *Naval and Military Record* and *Royal Dockyards Gazette*. The former at once took its place as the leading family weekly newspaper in the West of England; whilst the latter, has been lately enlarged and much improved and has now attained a larger circulation than any other Service paper.'

The Western Daily Mercury was started by Isaac Latimer in 1860.

Top left: *Advertisement for Cousins and exterior of his premises — patrons included the Duke and Duchess of Edinburgh, Prince Alfred of Edinburgh and the Duke of York.* Above top: *Early view of George Street prior to the construction of the Wiltshire and Dorset Bank as seen in the picture directly above.*

As we have already established, Union Street was laid out to provide better access to Plymouth from Stonehouse and Devonport. Previously there had been a substantial hill on the edge of the Sourpool at the back of Millbay and this had generally been negotiated via Stonehouse Lane, a route that was only 16 feet wide in some places and was not always regarded as smooth nor safe: 'it is not only inconveniently narrow, but constantly out of repair.' (PoP 1812)

A street of two halves, one in Plymouth and the other in Stonehouse, there was a ready demand for shops in the Stonehouse section as there had been no clear retail focal point for that community prior to the construction of Union Street. In Plymouth the demand was by no means as great and in the early days this stretch of the new route was largely populated with private residences.

The arrival of the railway and the development of Millbay Docks did much to alter the complexion of the neighbourhood. Union Street has perhaps undergone more rapid change in many respects, in the last 70 years than most, but by no means all, of our other major thoroughfares. The arrival of the tram has helped too; the route from Derry's Clock through Union Street was the first in Plymouth to be blessed with the service in 1872.

Top left: *Turning into Union Street from Bank of England Place.* Bottom left: *Looking down Union Street towards the railway bridge.* Above and left: *Henry Yeo's photographic studio in Union Street.*

150

Entirely straight, but for the dog-leg from George Street via Bank of England Place, Union Street supports a very diverse range of businesses, among them a number of public houses and hotels, foremost among them, Farley's Hotel, near the railway bridge: 'a comfortable commercial hotel, fitted in the most approved modern style.' (Wright 1879). This had been a private residence until the 1840s when Elizabeth Andrews converted it into a lodging house.

In the 1870s this well-situated hotel, whose rear elevation was overlooked by Millbay Station, was run by Charles Walter who made it his business to ensure that porters from the hotel met every train. Further expanded in the 1890s, it has become one of the Three Town's finer hotels and has an 80-foot-long commercial room, a 60-foot-long coffee room and an elegant billiard saloon. The expansion involved the demolition of the adjacent Birkhead Hotel.

Top left and right: Birkhead Hotel - Ebenezer Birkhead was here at the same time as Elizabeth Andrews. Above: Edward Penwill's Great Western Fancy Bazaar, toy and fancy good store in Union Street. Right: Walter's Farley Hotel viewed from the Union Street Bridge.

The gradual transformation of Union Street is at least partially well documented in the two photographs on the left here: one looking from the railway bridge, the other from a similar vantage point but at street level. See how the top image, taken by Francis Frith in 1889, differs dramatically from the bottom image. Within a decade or so the gardens of the residential properties on the right had been built out over and the shop units now extended out to the street line.

Frith had already built up a substantial collection of photo-pictures of the Plymouth area (and all around the country) by this stage. Countless towns and villages have reason to be grateful to this pioneer of topographical imagery and to Thomas Doidge who sold these pictures locally. Mr Doidge had bought the family business — then based in Whimple Street — in 1866, when he was 33 and the following year relocated to Union Street. Three years later he founded *Doidge's Western Counties Illustrated Annual*, which by the 1880s was 'the largest shilling annual in the world'.

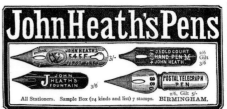

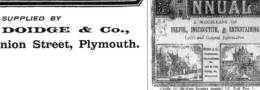

Top left: Union Street from the railway bridge in 1889. Above: The same view soon after electrification of the tram network.
Right: Advertisements for products available from Thomas Doidge's Union Street operation, including his celebrated Almanac.

Yield to Every Movement!
Are Genuine Supports!
Tough as Leather!
Soft as Silk!

Hartnoll's Corsets

Perfect in Shape!
Give Comfort and Style!
A Broken Spring Never Known!

The "NOLL-HART" (Trade Mark) CORSET.

3/11½ to One Guinea.
Post Free

ILLUSTRATED CATALOGUE SENT ON APPLICATION.

W. HARTNOLL,
Warwick House,
186, Union St., Plymouth.

Doidge's Western Counties Illustrated Annual. 65

Wm. DERRY & Co.,
Wine Merchants,
192, UNION STREET, PLYMOUTH.
Wines Packed by Experienced Packers.

WM. DERRY & Co.,
General Carriers.

Improved System for Removing Furniture, Pianos, Glass, China, Pictures, &c.

AGENTS FOR THE GREAT WESTERN RAILWAY.
192, UNION STREET, PLYMOUTH.

ESTIMATES FOR REMOVING . . .

Large or small Quantities of Furniture or Goods of any description to or from any part of the kingdom. . . . . .

Furniture Stored in Lock-up Warehouses.

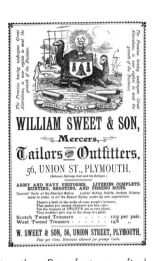

WILLIAM SWEET & SON,
Mercers,
Tailors and Outfitters,
56, UNION ST., PLYMOUTH.
(Between Railway Arch and the Octagon.)

ARMY AND NAVY UNIFORMS. LIVERIES COMPLETE.
HUNTING, SHOOTING, AND FISHING SUITS.

Tourists' Suits at the Shortest Notice. Ladies' Riding Habits, Jackets, Ulsters, made to order, in all the Newest Styles, under my own supervision.

There's a fault in the make of some people's trousers,
That makes you uneasy whenever you bow, sirs;
But the trousers at SWEET'S are so very pliant,
They wouldn't give way to the stoop of a giant.

Scotch Tweed Trousers - - - - 12/9 per pair.
West Tweed Trousers - - - - - 14/6   „

W. SWEET & SON, 56, UNION STREET, PLYMOUTH.
Five per Cent. Discount allowed for prompt Cash.

For the record, it isn't just shops that we have seen built out over the gardens of the houses on the northern side of Union Street for, diagonally opposite the Farley Hotel, on the other side of the railway bridge, the Beaufort Hotel was erected on the site of what had been the most westerly garden of Devonshire Terrace.

Next door to the Beaufort we find Sheppard's Arch Restaurant which, after the bridge was widened (compare the image in the middle on the right with that on the bottom left of this page), is about as close as you could possibly imagine a building to be to a busy railway line.

Top: *Advertisements for different Union Street businesses.* Right top: *Horse tram with the railway bridge in the distance.* Middle: *Before the bridge was widened.* Bottom and above right: *The Beaufort and Sheppard's Arrch Restaurant.* Above left: *Simonds Brewery at the Octagon.*

153

One of the more curious stories of recent years arose when the Corporation refused to grant the lease of the Theatre Royal to Henry Reed.

Reed's father-in-law, John Newcombe, actor and sportsman, had held the post of manager of the Theatre Royal for 42 years and in that time he had turned the place from a forlorn, loss-making enterprise into a highly successful concern. Newcombe was a well-known figure around town but was also known for his run-ins with his landlords, Plymouth Corporation.

Denied the opportunity to maintain momentum at the Theatre Royal, Henry Reed bought a large furnishing business in Union Street and in 16 weeks proceeded to convert the site into the largest building yet seen in the Stonehouse stretch of Union Street — the Grand Theatre.

With the biggest stage west of Bristol, it opened on Boxing Day 1889, with the pantomime 'Cinderella'.

It was an instant success, so successful in fact that Union Street consolidated its growing reputation as an entertainment centre, prompting London millionaire, Henry Pocock, and two travelling entertainers — the Livermore Brothers — to invest in the street.

As the United Counties Theatres Limited they brought the latest form of entertainment to the town in 1898 — Music Hall.

Bottom left: *Squire Terrace, Union Street, with the new Palace Theatre being the last property in Plymouth before crossing into Stonehouse.* Top: *The Star Inn, No. 8 Squire Terrace.* Above: *Inside the Palace Theatre.* Inset: *Posters for Grand's opening Panto and St James' Hall.*

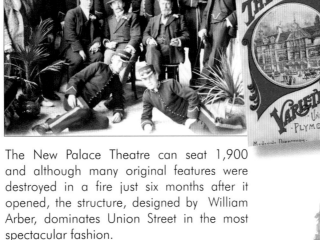

Firstly they bought out St James' Hall (already a popular venue) on the other side of Union Street, then they bought the site partly occupied by a 'Pandemonium' known as Fancy Fair. The building that arose on that footprint, on the corner of Union Street and Phoenix Street (the boundary with Stonehouse) has turned out to be, with the adjacent hotel, the largest investment to date (£185,000) in a private scheme West of Bristol.

The New Palace Theatre can seat 1,900 and although many original features were destroyed in a fire just six months after it opened, the structure, designed by William Arber, dominates Union Street in the most spectacular fashion.

Its wonderful façade is finished in hand-made tiles from Italy, two parts of which are covered in Sir Oswald Brierley's celebrated Armada battle scenes.

Top left and right: *Liveried staff at the opening of the New Palace Theatre.* Above: *One of HB Brewer's original murals for the Palace stage.* Right: *The splendid New Palace Theatre — note the Guildhall tower in the distance.*

Before we cross the Manor Street/Phoenix Street line into Stonehouse it is worth considering the impact that developments at Millbay have had on Plymouth — as well as Stonehouse and Devonport — over the last 50 years.

Certainly the arrival of the railway in 1849 was a red-letter day in the history of the Three Towns. Before the arrival of the steam train it would take 21¼ hours to get to London by the fastest coach on the road — the 'Quicksilver'; by train it could be done in nine hours.

In the 1890s ... 'leaving Plymouth at nine o'clock in the morning, we may reach London at 2.30, have time to transact our business in the City, and, leaving by the five o'clock from either Waterloo or Paddington, reach Plymouth again in time for supper. What would our forefathers have said to that?' asked William Wright in 1894.

Today there are nearly 150 passenger trains a day in and out of six major passenger stations operating out of the radius of the Three Towns, along with a proportionate number of goods stations.

Top left: *Millbay Station showing narrow and broad gauge lines together — the broad gauge lines were removed recently.*
Bottom left: *The Duke of Cornwall Hotel on the site of Mount Pleasant Grove.* Above: *A later view after the removal of Millbay Prison.*

The ease with which people and produce can be transported around the country has transformed the fortunes of all those able to stable the 'Iron Horse.' Commerce and tourism have benefitted enormously. Millbay has thrived, although the station itself has struggled to surpass its early status as a 'shabby shed' and in recent years has been somewhat eclipsed by a move to concentrate the main traffic of our railways a little more to the north and east of the town.

Architecturally, Millbay Station has been quite literally overshadowed by the Duke of Cornwall Hotel which stands directly opposite upon the site of the old 'Saracen's Head.' Here, in the 1840s sat Mount Pleasant Grove — 'a very charming row of houses, with a pretty little garden in front and only a footpath running along in front of the houses.' (Samuel Weekes)

The Duke itself was erected in 1865 from the designs of Mr Charles Hayward, the builders being Messrs Call & Pethick, the cost £40,000.

Close by, at the entrance to the station, we find the Albion Hotel, 'a square building of imposing appearance, now occupied and furnished as a commercial and family hotel, but recently occupied temporarily as railway offices by the late South Devon Railway Company. The general offices of the company adjoin the building, somewhat nearer the station.

Next to the Albion is the Eye Informary, one of the most useful institutions the town possesses. It was established in 1821.

Above: *Millbay Station.* Left: *Station with the Albion Hotel and later Continental Hotel in the distance.* Right: *Fowler's Albion Hotel* .

Heading in the opposite direction we come upon Millbay Barracks and Millbay Prisons on the corner across from the Duke of Cornwall.

'Erected towards the close of the last century, and used for the reception of the French prisoners, during the troublous times of the "great war" — these prisons are capable of accommodating about 3,000 men. The barracks were attached and are capable of holding 1,000 men. A depôt of one of the garrison regiments is constantly stationed here. The place is also used as the pay office of the pensioners of the army and navy.' (Wright 1879)

Meanwhile, 'on the other side of Millbay Road is the Mileage Yard, having communication with every part of the Docks. Close to the latter is the manufactory of the Millbay Soap Company, whilst nearer the Dock entrance is the establishment of the Victoria Soap Company.

'Soap Works are among the more important manufactures of Plymouth, and have become, in fact, one of the staple trades of the place.

'This manufacture was introduced in 1818 by Mr Thomas Gill and the works erected at Millbay. They were afterwards called the "Millbay Soap, Alkali and Soda Company." The Soda and Alkali Works were built about 1830, but are now discontinued, the very large premises being entirely devoted to the manufacture of soap. As large a quantity as 20 tons per hour can be produced in this establishment. The speciality of these important works is called the "Millbay Soap", and the bars are marked with the arms of Plymouth and the name "Millbay".

'The Victoria Soap Works are also very extensive. The Victoria Soap Company was established in 1858, by Mr FA Morrish, and, in 1863, the "West of England Soap Company" was purchased, together with the plant and removed from Sutton Road. Their great speciality is toilet soap and at the Exhibition of 1862 they had the medal for excellence of quality awarded.' (Wright 1879)

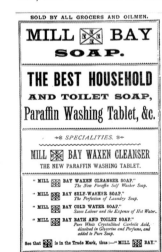

Top left: *The junction of Citadel Road and Millbay Road looking across to Millbay Prison.* Middle: *The same view from a different angle.* Bottom: *Further around towards Millbay.* Left: *Millbay Soap advert from 1890.* Above: *Millbay Road offices of the hugely successful Western Counties' Agricultural Co-operative Association.*

Millbay's story is indeed a remarkable one: 'As the town grew in importance, so the desirability of turning the capacious inlet of Millbay to account became apparent ... Millbay was the resort of vessels, which were accustomed to lie where the Octagon now is. The first attempt of importance to provide special accommodation was made in the formation of the Union Dock, of which Mr WH Evens and the Messrs. Derry were the promoters, in what is now the southern angle, between Martin and Phoenix Street.

Subsequently, in 1839, Mr Thomas Gill laid a project for the erection of Millbay Pier ... and the Pier was built and a dock adjoining. The next step was the formation of the Great Western Docks Company, and Mr Brunel was appointed engineer of the Docks. In February 1857 the floating basin was opened. One of the chief advantages of the Docks is their deep water approach. Extensive warehouses have, from time to time, been added. A line of railway runs around the wharves.' (RN Worth 1871)

Top left: *Treleaven Coal warehouse MIllbay.* Top right: *Fox Elliott's timber operation at Millbay.* Above: *General view of the Docks looking east.*

The Royal William Victualling Yard c1868.

STONEHOUSE AND STOKE

Stonehouse has been heavily reliant on Government institutions since the construction of the Royal Naval Hospital in the second half of last century. The arrival of the Royal Marines a decade or two later and then the erection of the Military Hospital on the other side of Stonehouse Creek in the 1790s, all added to that dependency. The whole of this was compounded, at the beginning of this century, with the massive investment that saw the creation of the Royal William Victualling Yard — without doubt the grandest and most impressive of the projects to date.

Inside the Royal Marine Barracks c1898.

Durnford Street and the Royal Marine Barracks c1894

In addition to the great number of servicemen based in and around the Stonehouse peninsula, there are also a considerable number of sizeable businesses and manufactories, among them the Valletort Steam Laundry and several breweries: foremost among them, Plymouth Breweries at the end of Chapel Street.

In 1850 Stonehouse acquired what is perhaps the most important community building, in the shape of St George's Hall. 'This is used as a townhall and for public meetings, lectures, assemblies, concerts, &c. It was designed by Messrs. Fuller & Gingell, of Bristol, and built by Thomas Clift & Co., of Martin Street.

The cost of erection was £4,250, exclusive of the land and the stone of which it was built, which were the gifts of the Earl of Mount Edgcumbe.' *(Wright 1879)*

'We next proceed to an inspection of St George's Parish Church, in Chapel Street. The building was erected in 1789, by subscription, on the site of an ancient chapel.

'Since the succession of Rev Percy Scott, MA, an energetic movement has been started for the purpose of restoring the Church, and some fruits are already visible. A handsome chancel window has been fixed by Mr Fouracre, a new organ erected by Messrs. Hele Bros., and other improvements effected.

'Passing down Chapel Street, we notice, a door or two below St George's Church, the establishment of Messrs. Fouracre & Son.

'Messrs. Fouracre had set foot on a branch of art industry, entirely new to this locality, namely the painting and staining of glass, and the design and manufacture of stained windows.

Top left: *Advertisement for the Valletort Laundry.* Middle: *Exterior of Messrs. Fouracre's business.* Right: *Interior of St George's Church.* Above left and middle: *Plymouth Breweries.* Above right: *Offices of Pomeroy & Co., Ironmongers, at No.1 Edgcumbe Street.*

'Several of the windows in the New Guildhall, and a portion of the artistic embellishments of St Andrew's Church, as well as of other buildings, have been executed by this firm.' *(Wright 1879)*

'At the far end of the Peninsula we find the Winter Villa, one of the residences of the Earl of Mount Edgcumbe: but now inhabited from time to time by noblemen and others who may be making a brief term of residence in this locality.' *(Ibid)*

There is, incidentally, a regular ferry service between Admiral's Hard, and Cremyll Passage, the landing-place for Mount Edgcumbe. 'Here, especially on Wednesdays, during the summer months, may be witnessed some lively scenes; for crowds of people pass and repass to the boats, which convey them to and fro; the trip to Mount Edgcumbe being considered as one of the treats of the season by all classes of the population; for it must be borne in mind that the noble Earl opens his beautiful grounds free to all-comers once a week.'

The ferry provides a sea view of the Royal William Victualling Yard, 'the most important establishment in the township, and one of the principal public establishments of the district. It is a magnificent pile of buildings, erected at a cost of a million and a half of money, and covering no less than 13 acres of ground.' *(ibid)*

Top right: *Winter Villa former residence of the Edgcumbe family.*
Above: *Stonehall, another former Edgcumbe residence.*
Right: *Admiral's Hard.*

We have now taken a look at two of the principal routes in and out of Stonehouse, via Union Street and the Cremyll Ferry. There are also two bridges, Millbridge and Stonehouse Bridge. The latter was constructed to the designs of John Smeaton, he of the Eddystone Light fame, and was completed in 1773. The Earl of Mount Edgcumbe and Sir John St Aubyn were joint proprietors.

'Toll is paid by all foot passengers (except soldiers) as well as for vehicles and animals, and the bridge, by this means, produces a large sum annually. It is let by contract yearly at a very high rental. "Halfpenny Gate," as it is known, has become a long-standing grievance of these towns, and one which ought to be abolished in these days of free communication and opening up of public roads.' (Wright 1879)

As the route over Stonehouse Bridge saw the first tram lines laid out in this area it was also where 'trace' or 'chain' horses were first deployed to help the work of pulling trams up the challenging incline of Devonport Hill.

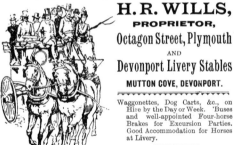

OCTAGON MEWS.

H. R. WILLS,
PROPRIETOR,
Octagon Street, Plymouth
AND
Devonport Livery Stables

MUTTON COVE, DEVONPORT.

Waggonettes, Dog Carts, &c., on Hire by the Day or Week. 'Buses and well-appointed Four-horse Brakes for Excursion Parties. Good Accommodation for Horses at Livery.

Hearses and Mourning Carriages.
Funeral Cars. Private Landaus.

Ordinarily the trams would have two horses on level ground and two others would be attached at Edgcumbe Place, with another one or two at Richmond Walk.

At the top of the hill the extra horses would be led, usually by a young lad — a trace boy — back to the depôt off Manor Lane, just north of Union Street. Here there were tram sheds and stabling for 116 horses.

The service started each weekday at 8.30am and ran until 10.30pm.

The Stonehouse Company's service didn't run on Sunday mornings, starting only at 1.15pm and finishing at the slightly earlier time of 10.15pm. At peak times, between 10am and 9pm, the service operated every five minutes. Outside of those hours it was every ten minutes. The maximum fare between Plymouth and Devonport was then 3d and tuppence ha'penny if you travelled outside. Between Plymouth and Edgcumbe Street, the fare was half that, but it was 2d from Stonehouse to Devonport.

A few years ago, and prior to the electrification of the system there was a bitter fallout between the directors of the tram company and the General Toll Company. It had been the custom for the tram-boy, when leading the three trace horses back to Manor Lane, to pay a lower rate at the toll gate, but for some reason the Toll Company, in 1895, took exception to the arrangement. Happily it was eventually resolved by making an overall adjustment to the amount paid by the Tram Company.

Top: *Stonehouse Bridge from the Quay.* Middle: *View from the bridge looking back down Edgcumbe Street.* ottom: *A trace-boy encourages his charges up Devonport Hill.*

Top: *Stonehouse Creek and the MIlitary Hospital.* Bottom left: *Hospital and Stoke Damerel Church.* Bottom right: *Victoria Park.*

The other principal route in and out of Stonehouse, as we have already alluded to, was via Millbridge, a byway not favoured by the tram system doubtless on account of the steepness of Eldad Hill.

'As we prepare to descend the hill at Eldad, leaving North Road to our right, we notice the Albert Hall, for a short time a fashionable place of assemblage; where oratories and grand concerts were given, but owing to the bad approaches, it was never a favourite resort; and on the erection of the New Guildhall, it was quite superseded. It will hold about 3,000 people, being now used by circus companies, or for pedestrian matches. It has also done duty as a skating rink.

'At the foot of the hill we enter on the Millbridge, with its old mill still at work; for the special benefit of which the large sheet of water on the right is let in and out daily.

'On the other side of the bridge is a small neat chapel recently erected by the Primitive Methodists.

'By continuing the straight road before us, a pleasant ramble may be enjoyed amongst the villa-residences of Stoke, the grounds of which are, for the most part, tastefully kept. Several enclosed residences may also be found, with here and there a terrace, but except at the upper portion (Higher Stoke) there are but few business houses.

'Taking the road to the left we reach Stoke Church. The Parish Church of Stoke Damerel is of ancient foundation, but it has been considerably altered by successive enlargements, and there appears to be nothing of the original fabric left but the tower.

'The Church is picturesquely situated upon an eminence and is surrounded by an extensive graveyard.

'The interior is comfortably fitted up, and will accommodate about 800 persons. It has an organ and an efficient choir. The present rector is the Rev William St Aubyn, BA, the living being in the gift of the St Aubyn family, the present head of that family being the Lord of the Manor.

'Opposite Stoke Church is one of the most prominent objects in the neighbourhood, the Military Hospital erected in 1797.

Top left: *The old mill, 1899.* Middle: *Stoke Damerel Church from the burial yard 1899.* Bottom: *The Toll Gate at Millbridge.* Above: *Looking west from the junction of Fellowes Place and Wilton Street*

During the 1890s the upper part of Stonehouse Creek has been infilled, primarily for recreation purposes for the benefit of the young lads of the Three Towns, but clearly the girls enjoy it too.

'We now cross a substantial bridge, recently erected by the London & South Western Railway Company, to the Railway Station, the headquarters of the Narrow Gauge Extension in the West of England.

'It is a handsome structure and possesses superior accommodation both for passengers and for goods traffic. In connection therewith is a branch line which passes under the road from Stonehouse to Devonport, and is designed to communicate with the Devonport side of Stonehouse Pool. An iron footbridge near the Church conducts to Waterloo Street and thence to Devonport Park.' *(Wright 1879)*

'Rented by the Corporation from the War Office, Devonport Park is being gradually laid out, with walks, trees, shrubs, arbours, seats, &c., and affords at once a splendid recreation ground, and fine promenade, with a beautiful view of the surrounding scenery. Here the grand review upon her Majesty's birthday is held, when all the troops in the garrison and volunteers from many towns around assemble, the sight being brilliant, and the concourse of people very great.'*(Chatty Joe 1874)*

The Park, one of the first in the area, was begun in the late 1850s, the little Swiss Lodge at the entrance being erected in 1858. The Swiss-style was a popular one at the time following the fashion set by Prince Albert.

The Park has been further developed in the 1890s, most notably with the construction of the very distinctive Park Pavilion.

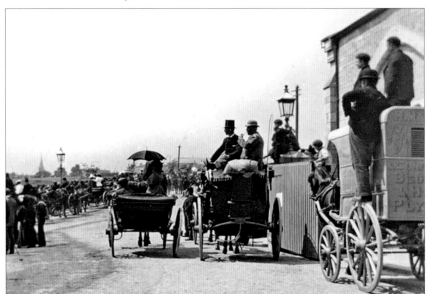

Top Left: *The Devonport and Stonehouse Railway Station, was opened on 17 May 1876.* Middle: *Inside the station c1890 — the Broad Gauge service ended in May 1892.* Bottom: *Looking across the Brickfields to the station during a major review, c1895.* Above: *View from the station.*

DEVONPORT

A new electric tram makes its way towards Fore Street, Devonport, past the Park. Inset top: The Devonport Technical Schools opened in 1899. Designed by HJ Snell, the building has fine stained glass windows by Fouracre depicting the development of naval architecture through the career of Devonport-born Sir William White (Chief Constructor of the Navy). Right: Devonport Park Fountain, erected to the memory of Sir Charles Napier.

Watermen with their boats at Mutton Cove.

Well into the present century, landward entry into the town of Devonport (or Plymouth Dock as it was known until 1824) was via three drawbridges: at the top of Devonport Hill, the top of New Passage Hill, and the entrance to Fore Street.

By boat, apart from official business into Mount Wise, the Dockyard or the railway terminal at Ocean Quay (at the end of Richmond Walk), there are two principal access points: at North Corner and at Mutton Cove.

'This is the chief place of embarkation and debarkation of seamen and others to or from the ships in the Sound, and also the nearest point to Cremyll, on the Mount Edgcumbe shore.

'Owing to its proximity to the mouth of the harbour, Mutton Cove is often exposed to heavy seas; consequently, the landing place has been sheltered by piers running out from either side.

'The view from this point is interesting in the extreme, although a little higher, at Mount Wise, one of the finest views in the district may be obtained.' *(Wright 1879)*

Although perhaps not as busy as it has been in the past, Mutton Cove still supports a lively community of watermen and watering-holes, among them the Mount Edgcumbe Inn, the Mutton Cove Hotel and the recently closed Waterman's Arms.

George Sibley, the landlord of the Mutton Cove Hotel, also has a thriving wagonette business, and his handsome horses with their shiny coats are regularly seen drawing their fine coaches all around the area. Johnston Beck and JW Nichols are the Pier Masters here and the Cove is replete with its own Custom House, Boarding Station and Bonded Stores.

The other principal businesses here are centred mainly around the discharging of coal with William Bennett operating one of the larger local concerns out of Bullock's Dock.

In the distant past it seems that the harbour had something of a reputation as a favourite haunt for smugglers. Not that many years ago (in 1873), two Mutton Cove watermen, William Kendall and Richard Neptune were charged with smuggling 97lbs of tobacco stalks. Kendall claimed that the stalks had come from the troopship *Tamar* but that he couldn't identify the man who had given them to him. 'The bench fined the defendants £100 or six months' imprisonment, this being the lowest penalty the Commissioners of Customs could inflict. The men went to gaol.' *(WMN 28 February 1873)*

Top: *Trippers accessing boats at Mutton Cove.* Bottom: *Servicemen outside Mark Hollow's Edgcumbe Inn.*

'A short distance from Mutton Cove is Pembroke Street with a turning into George Street, where we find St Stephen's Church, erected in 1852, from the designs of Mr St Aubyn. The Church affords accommodation for 764 persons and the service may be designated as "high."

'At the extremity of George Street, on our right, as we leave the street, is Admiralty House, the official residence of the Port Admiral, with offices attached. In front is Government House, the official residence of the General Commanding the Western District.

'On the extensive parade ground are frequently held Military inspections and parades. Near the front of Government House is a large brass cannon, which was captured from the Turks in the Dardanelles. Near the fort is a fine statue of John Colborne, Baron Seaton, born 1788, died 1863. The sculptor was Mr Adams, and the founders Messrs. Elkington. It was a gift to the town, having been offered to and rejected by the authorities of the town of Plymouth.

Above: *Statue of John Colborne, Baron Seaton in front of Government House, Mount Wise.* Top: *Government House.* Bottom right: *Admiralty House.*

'On the hill, at the west end of the parade, is the Semaphore and signal station, from which signals are made with any vessels of the Royal Navy in the Sound or passing up and down the Channel.

'Around us are ramparts and batteries, mounted with heavy artillery, intended for the defence of the Dockyard and the other costly national establishments in the neighbourhood.

'By taking the path to the south and descending the steep eminence, we reach the "Queen's Stairs," a landing pier for the convenience of persons employing watermen's boats, from whence passage may be taken to Mount Edgcumbe, Millbrook, &c., &c., A little to the left are the Royal Clarence Baths, situated in a charming nook.

'Here hot and cold baths and sea bathing may be indulged in, with convenient bathing machines provided for those desiring their use.

'From the Baths, a path leads past the trenches surrounding the batteries, to Richmond Walk, a fine promenade, formed by the Duke of that name.' *(W 1879)*

Top left: *Mount Wise and HMS Neptune from the water.*
Top right: *The Signalling Station.*
Middle right: *Royal Clarence Baths.*
Right: *1889 Laboratory House, Mount Wise, which was attached to the Royal Laboratory built for the Board of Ordnance in 1805 for the manufacture of musket cartridges and other ammunition and explosive devices such as rockets for the Navy.*
Far right: *Group outside the house in July 1889.*

Above: The view from the Column looking south-west. Foulston's Ker Street terrace is in the foreground and St Stephen's Church at the end of George Street on the right.

The name 'Devonport' was conferred upon Plymouth Dock in 1824 and, to celebrate their independence from Plymouth, the townspeople commissioned John Foulston to create a victory column alongside their newly completed (1821) Town Hall.

'The column was erected by Mr Richard, the builder of the Town Hall and it is curious to note that the structure was raised without the aid of any exterior scaffolding.

'Within it is a spiral staircase, leading to a balcony on the summit of the capital. This is surrounded by an iron railing, and commands an extensive and delightful prospect.

'The flagstaff on the Column is used for hoisting the weather signal for watermen — one red triangular flag denoting "stormy," double fare being then payable; and two flags denoting "tempestuous," when special terms must be made.

'To the right of the Column is the Mount Zion Chapel. It is designed after the Hindoo style and erected 1823-4. Adjoining the chapel is the building formerly used as a Public Library, but now as an Odd-Fellows' Hall. It was erected in 1833, from the designs of Mr Foulston, and is in the Egyptian style of architecture.

Above: *John Foulston's varied collection at the top of Ker Street. Town Hall, Column, Zion Chapel and Odd Fellows' Hall.*
Left: *View from Devonport Column looking north east, with St Aubyn Church and Raglan Barracks in the middle distance.*

'Raglan Barracks cover an area of some 11 acres, 3½ of which are covered with buildings, and 4½ acres are taken up by the Parade. They are constructed to accommodate two entire regiments of the Line, or 2,000 men and 80 officers. The barracks occupy the sites of the old Frederick, Ligonier, and Cumberland Squares, together with portions of Picquet Barracks and St George's Square.

'On the eastern side of the Parade stands the principal entrance building which is built in the Doric style of limestone with granite dressings, and flat roof covered with asphalt, surmounted with a clock-tower, having a clock with four dials, for use of the garrison. 'All the other buildings are built with grey stock bricks above their basements which are limestone, and all have granite dressings.'

Left: *Devonport Market from the Column. The clock tower with roof and vane are 124ft in height.*
Above: Looking up Tavistock Street.
Below: *Looking down Cumberland Street towards the Market.*
Opposite page top: *Roglan Barracks from the Lines.*
Middle: *Drill practice.* Bottom: *On Parade, 1896.*

Also sporting a clock with four dials is the tower of Devonport Market, 'one of the more noticeable objects in the view of the town.

'The market is the property of the Lord of the Manor, and was erected in 1852, from the designs of Mr JP St Aubyn, at a cost of £20,000.

'The principal front is in Tavistock Street from which we enter, but there are also entrances from Catherine Street, Pond Lane, and Duke Street.

'We first enter the fish market, next to the vegetable market, and, on the other side of the yard, the butchery and shops. In the centre is a staircase leading to the upper floor and store rooms.

'The nearby Mechanics Institute in Duke Street has, at present, the largest public room in Devonport. The lecture hall will accommodate 1,000 persons, and an excellent prospectus of lectures is provided every winter, with occasional concerts and entertainments.

'Dramatic representations are also frequently given, there being at present no licensed theatre in the town. Josiah Clark is the resident librarian.' *(Wright 1879)*

If the advent of steam has had a major impact on land travel during our present century, it should not be imagined that it has had any less of an effect on sea travel and the design of our seagoing vessels. An obvious consequence of this, of course, has been a series of major changes to the arrangements in the Dockyard itself, most notably with the construction of Keyham Steamyard and with changes from sail to steam and from wood to steel.

No longer is there a requirement for large stacks of oak timber to be kept in open sheds until seasoned.

No longer is there need for big old saw-pits. In the late-1850s new smaller sawmills were built to meet the reduced demand.

Demand that has decreased yet further as the century has progressed, it is, in many ways a saga that is best told through the story of two oceans.

On 23 August 1860 work began in Devonport on the construction of the new, wooden, line-of-battle ship HMS *Ocean*. Before long however, the Admiralty directed that — along with her sister ships *Prince Consort*, *Caledonia* and *Royal Alfred* — she be converted into an iron-clad.

Thus *Ocean* became the first armour-plated ship to be built in the Dockyard and, after 22 years of service around the world, she was broken up.

Moving our clock forward to the Queen's Jubilee Year, 1897, after No.3 dock had been extended the previous year, work began on the second HMS *Ocean* to be built in Devonport (and the fourth Royal Naval vessel of that name).

During the construction there was a major setback when two gangs of men were called away to help dock the battleship *Colossus*.

Suddenly the ribs of the ship fell away and some 90 feet of the fore part of the ship, amounting to around 100 tons of material, collapsed. All of it the fault of a simple error by one of the labourers.

Notwithstanding a few other vexatious delays, *Ocean* was eventually launched on 5 July 1898, and although not the heaviest ship ever launched, she was heavier per foot length than any other ship previously launched in a Royal Naval Dockyard.

HRH Princess Louise, the guest of the Earl of Mount Edgcumbe, officiated and 'an enormous crowd of visitors from many parts of the West of England, estimated at 30,000, assembled in the Dockyard to witness the event.'

One of the Canopus-class battleships, she was designed by locally born Sir William White.

Opposite page top and bottom: *General views of Devonport Dockyard.* Top left and middle: *5 July 1898 launch of HMS* Ocean. Above: *The Terrace with the Admiral's House.*

Within the Lines and outside of the Dockyard walls the streets of Devonport tell a number of different stories — some more healthy and wholesome than others.

Marlborough Street is one of the chief business thoroughfares in the town and is but a short distance from Morice Square where we find St Paul's Church, built in 1849 from the designs of Mr St Aubyn, as well as a large Baptist chapel, and, in Morice Street itself, a chapel of the Wesleyan Methodists.

At the back of Morice Square conditions were a little less inviting. In 1895, Henry Whitfeld addressed an open letter to the Lady of the Manor, entitled 'The Boy From The Back of Morice Square'. The pathetic revelations revealed in the document led to the formation of the Dockyard Dwellings Company. Part of the problem had traditionally been that as most of the properties in Devonport were owned by the St Aubyn family and let on the basis of 'three lives' tenancies, there was little incentive to look after the said dwellings.

Top left: *Pitcher's House Decorators premises in Marlborough Street — the firm have large orders from the Admiralty and the Corporation.*
Top right: *James Street.* Left: *St Paul's, Morice Square.* Above: *Morice Square Baptist outing.*

The principle of the 'three lives' was that the leaseholder would list his own name and that of two others, generally children, to whom the lease would pass and that on the death of the last named individual the property would return to the Lord of the Manor.

It was not a good system, particularly in the light of comments made some years earlier, in 1882, by the Lord of Manor, when he said that it was a bad thing when the desire to build was greater than the demand for houses, and houses became tenanted by a class of persons lower than those for whom they were intended.

In 1897 Mr Whitfeld produced another pamphlet — 'The Curse of Devonport' — and in one day alone some 12,000 copies were sold.

'Proceeding systematically through the borough slums, I could not fail to be impressed with those recurring views of ruined and collapsed houses which a casual visitor from a volcanic country might be excused for regarding as the evidences of a nineteenth-century earthquake.

'Whilst Plymouth, has still its overcrowding evils, and is trying to cure them, the Manorial System of Devonport results in structural decay and public indifference.

'The sanitary aspect, in truth, is almost inferior to the commercial consequences of that Leasehold Curse which has so long hung over the borough like a depressing cloud. Without malice, and extenuating nothing, the facts have been set forth, in the hope that revelation may be followed by reform so comprehensive and complete that Devonport may not only vie with Plymouth in the application of social remedies in the interest of the poor, but may prevail upon the Manor Authorities to loosen that uncommercial grasp on available sites which has for years been the cause of impoverishment to nearly every class of its community by giving the land in the area a purely arbitrary value.'

Top left: *James Street*. Middle and right: *Back of Morice Square*. Above: *Rear of James Street, all images 1895*.

By contrast, 'Fore Street has a fine appearance, many of the buildings being of a superior order, and the business establishments of a first-class character. Prominent amongst them will be noticed the newly fronted and improved Royal Hotel, and the United Services Club adjoining.

'The Royal Hotel is the largest house of the kind in Devonport, and possesses some fine rooms, particularly the new dining-rooms, where banquets, balls and dinners are frequently held.'

Close by the Dockyard Gate is Agnes Weston's Royal Sailor's Rest. From humble origins, offering 'Coffee, Comfort and Company,' all for a penny.

Top left: *1870s construction work on expanding Agnes Weston's Sailor's Rest.*
Top right: *The Dockyard Gates.* Above: *General view of Fore Street towards the gates with further expansion to the Sailor's Rest.* Right: *Fore Street c1892.*

This noble and temperate institution was established here in the 1870s and expanded massively in the late 1880s, taking in the whole of the Fore Street/Edinburgh Road corner site.

The Devonport Bank is also a noticeable building. There are also branches of the National Provincial Bank of England and the Devon & Cornwall Bank in this street.

'The Post Office at the top of Chapel Street is a fine building, in the Classical style; and was erected in 1849, from the designs of Mr George Wightwick.

'The Temperance Hall is the next building that attracts our attention, it was opened in 1850, the architect being Mr JP St Aubyn.

'Passing on we reach the bridge over the wide trench which surrounds the town of Devonport, and where, until recently, stood massive granite arches, with draw-bridge attached. These arches (with trenches and ramparts extending the whole circuit of the town landwards) were portions of the scheme of fortification commenced early in the present century and suspended in 1816, but recommenced and completed in 1853; and as far as the three main entrances were concerned, removed within the last 10 years.'

Top left: Royal Hotel first corner on the left. Top right: The Temperance Hall is in the distance on the left. Above: Devonport Post Office, built as an adaptation of the Temple of Tivoli. Left: 102 Fore Street, Albert Pengelly's tobacconists.

At the top of New Passage Hill, where was sited one of the three entrances to the town, we find the Royal Albert Hospital.

'This building was erected in 1862-3 from the designs of Mr A Norman, in the Italian style, at a cost of £11,500, raised partly by subscription and partly by grants from the Admiralty and the War Office.

'This institution is of great value, for previous to its erection the only hospital in the district was at Plymouth. The western portion of the building is a general public hospital and contains accident wards, male and female general wards and special wards for particular diseases. It also has a children's ward and eye infirmary.

'A provident dispensary is also attached to the Hospital. The east wing, which has a separate entrance, is a Lock hospital, erected and maintained by the Government.

The West of England Pianoforte Saloons.

❖ P. A. NORMAN, ❖

Importer of English & Foreign Musical Instruments
OF EVERY DESCRIPTION.

PIANOS

SALE, ❖ HIRE,

3 Years' System,

DELIVERED FREE TO ANY ADDRESS ON RECEIPT OF FIRST INSTALMENT.

~ TUNING. ~

Experienced Tuners visit all towns between Exeter and Penzance periodically or specially, if required.

N.B.
The Finest Stock of Instruments in the West.

16 ( ) ALBERT ROAD, MORICE TOWN, nr. DEVONPORT

'It provides for 62 patients in the general department, and 160 in the lock ward. From this it can be seen that the principal concern is the Lock hospital and that is primarily for the treatment, physical and mental, of fallen women and sexually transmitted diseases and is designed to curb the spread of such diseases among our servicemen.' *(W 1879)*
At the bottom of New Passage Hill is William Street. At the end of that is the entrance to the Keyham Steam Yard and the principal thoroughfare in Morice Town, Albert Road, not long since known as Navy Row.

Top left: *17 June 1862, the Earl of Mount Edgcumbe lays the foundation stone of the Royal Albert Hospital.* Bottom and middle: *Two views of the completed hospital.* Top right: *Advert for Norman's music store in Albert Road.* Middle: *Albert Road.* Bottom: *Fowler's Dental Practice — Nitrous oxide, cocaine or aether is used on approved subjects.*

Far left: *The Eagle Brewery, 1894.*
Left: *North Corner from the landing jetty.*
Below: *The Landing Jetty at the bottom of Cornwall Street (note the Piermaster's House). North Corner, just beyond the north wall of the Dockyard, was the first street to be laid out after work began on the King's New Dock.*

Before descending New Passage Hill, if we make a detour to the west, we pass through Queen Street and one of the more advanced breweries in the area: 'the system works as nearly automatically as ingenuity can make it and the Eagle Brewery Company's beers enjoy a well-earned popularity in the town and district.

'Meanwhile at the foot of Cornwall Street, or North Corner, is one of the principal public landing places in Devonport, where the river steamers embark their passengers and market produce, and where "Jack" may be found "ashore" in all stages of impressibility.

'Of old this was the favourite camping ground of press gangs on the one hand, and of land-sharks and crimps on the other, and "Poor Jack" was singularly fortunate if he could steer clear of the latter, as was the unsuspecting landsman of the former.'

The area around North Corner was originally inhabited by Dockyard workers and their families. Across the water, Torpoint, 'a little spreading town' is much the same, being 'tenanted principally by present or past dockyard or naval employees.'

The steam-driven Torpoint Floating Bridge was first introduced in 1834, with a second coming on stream the following year.

With a lamp on each corner the new ferry (shown left) crossed the Tamar four times an hour, taking eight minutes at high tide and four minutes at low tide.

Each was capable of carrying three four-horse carriages, one pair-horse carriage, seven saddle horses and 60 foot-passengers. These two continued in service until they were replaced in the 1870s.

The first of the two new Willoughby Brothers-built vessels came into service in 1871 and was distinguished by it's tall single funnel, while the second, with two funnels, was introduced at midday on Saturday 26 October 1878. Both of these ferries are still in service.

WESTERN COUNTIES'
MANURE COMPANY,

Torpoint, Devonport,

JOSEPH SHEPHEARD, Manager.

The above Company have for 30 years been before the public, and have earned a high reputation for the

HIGH CHARACTER OF THEIR MANURES.

THE COMPANY HAVE RECEIVED

THOUSANDS OF TESTIMONIALS

From various parts of the United Kingdom as to the efficiency of the Manures, and they can confidently appeal to their Customers as to the genuineness of the articles manufactured and the great success that has attended their use.

THE "SPECIAL"

Is a manure of a very high class, containing as it does **over 26 per cent. Soluble Phosphate, and over 5 per cent. Ammonia.**

THE DISSOLVED BONE

Is manufactured from Raw Bone and not from Burnt Bone or Burnt Ash, and it is from this fact that this article has given such

UNIVERSAL SUCCESS IN THE FIELD.

PRICES ON APPLICATION.

350

Top: *One of the two steam ferries brought into service at Torpoint in the 1830s. Both were replaced in the 1870s (see middle, bottom and right).*
Above right: *An advertisement for the Western Counties manure Company, a large establishment a little southward of Torpoint, established in 1854.*

Leaving Cornwall and back on the other side of the river '... It is admitted on all sides that the brewing trade in Devonshire is in a high state of perfection, and it will also be readily admitted that one of the best representatives in connection therewith is the Tamar Brewery, Morice Town.

'This concern has been in active existence for upwards of a century, and has achieved an excellent and widespread reputation for the uniform purity and high quality of its productions, and on these merits a steadily and rapidly increasing trade has been experienced. This fact is amply substantiated by the renown that the ales brewed here have won.

'The brewery — which is the freehold property of its present proprietor, Mr George Crake — is an establishment of large extent, covering a considerable area, and comprising the yards, offices, stores, malt-houses, hop-stores, and all other outbuildings; extensive and important structural alterations having been recently completed, adding considerably to the buildings. Each department is admirably arranged and equipped for its special purpose in the routine of the industry, and the entire premises present an example of good organisation, denoting careful management, enterprise, and experience on the part of the proprietor and the staff.' *(W 1894)*

Also based in Morice Town, with haulage plant and wharfage accommodations for vessels up to 1,200 tons, are Messrs Harvey & Son, one of the leading, most representative and probably the oldest in the trade, having been established upwards of fifty years ago. The firm are purveyors of the 'black diamond of general utility', coal ... a necessity to the rich and poor — the manufacturer, general tradesman and the private individual.'

Corn is another commodity that Harvey & Son sell in great quantities.

'In both sections of the business a large trade is carried on, and contracts of considerable extent are entered into with the Army and Navy.' *(ibid)*

Top left and middle: Inside and outside of the Tamar Brewery. Top right: The waterside premises of Harvey & Son.
Left: Looking back to Devonport from Torpoint and the chain-lined banks of the Tamar. Above right: St Levan viaduct.

Harvey & Son's base is off Pottery Quay, the Tamar Brewery is off the next inlet to the north, Tamar Canal, while the next inlet up is Moon Cove, above which we find Keyham Steam Yard.

In the early years of steam Devonport Dockyard fell a little behind Portsmouth and Woolwich but in the 1840s it was decided to build an entirely new yard accommodating the advances in engineering.

After surveying both sides of the Tamar a site was chosen and 38 acres of land and 43 acres of foreshore were purchased from the trustees of the will of Sir I St Aubyn.

'Here it is proposed to construct two floating basins about six acres each, with entrances 80 feet wide, laid at a depth sufficient for the largest steamer to enter and depart at all times of the tide.

'There are to be completed engine and boiler workshops, with the requisite tools and storehouses for fitting-out and repairing large fleets of steamers; the whole establishment will cover a surface of about 72 acres.' (Sir John Rennie)

In the event the Engineering Department was designed by Charles Barry (who had designed the Houses of Parliament in 1836) and by the time the yard was finished it was not only 'considerably larger than the one at Woolwich', but it was reckoned to be 'the finest and most extensive establishment of its kind in the kingdom.'

Water was first let into the Docks and Basins nine years after the contract had been awarded back in 1844, but it wasn't until 7 October 1853 that the Steam Yard was officially opened when HMS Queen was taken into the basin.

Top: HMS Queen and HMS Duke of Wellington were the first visitors to Keyham Steam Yard in 1853.
Left: Keyham's early fire service c1863.

'Prominent among the recent additions to the public buildings at Keyham Dockyard, the new Quarters for Engineer Students must also be counted as a noteworthy building for the sightseer. It is a large and handsome edifice, situated at the northern end of the yard, adjoining the officers' quarters and looking down over the engine and boiler shops from the rocky height adjoining the Saltash Road. It is a great addition to the attractions of the vicinity, and will compare favourably with any other public buildings in the West of England.' (W 1879)

'The Royal Naval Barracks at Devonport consist of a fine and substantially built group of stone buildings, and as viewed from the higher ground on the right of the road by which they are approached — as in the photograph above — present a pleasing picture. They lie at the present extremity of Keyham Dockyard, which is in the process of being considerably extended, the ground between the barracks and the harbour being just now a wilderness given over to the contractor, whose plant and crazy-looking little waggons are very much in evidence.' (A&NI 1897)

Top left: *Royal Naval Engineering College, Keyham*. Top right: *Royal Naval Barracks*. Bottom left: *Keyham Extension works looking towards Barne Barton*. Above right: *Work progressing on the Keyham extension, note the viaduct over Camel's Head Creek in the distance.*

CAMEL'S HEAD, ST BUDEAUX AND BEYOND

'By continuing our tour north, Camel's Head will be reached; at which point the Cornish Railway runs over the Keyham Lake, by the Camel's Head Viaduct. There is also a bridge for foot passengers and vehicles.'

Not everyone, however, takes heed of the difference: 'A sad accident occurred on the Cornwall Railway on Saturday afternoon (18 September 1869). Three little boys about nine years of age had been out picking blackberries, and returned home across the Camel's Head Viaduct. When half way across it, a train approaching warned them by its whistle of their danger, they heard it and took refuge in the manhole.

'One of them however, named Crenes, the son of a warrant officer, becoming frightened at the approach of the train jumped out and ran along the line. He was of course soon overtaken by the engine and knocked down, the wheels passed over both legs between the knee cutting them clean off, his thighs were also very much lacerated, and his left arm was broken.

'The train was stopped, and the passengers gave all the assistance they could to the poor little fellow. A door was obtained from a neighbouring farm, and he was conveyed to the Royal Albert Hospital, Devonport, where sensible to the last, he died two hours after his admission.' (IT 1869)

For some, sadly, the water was no safer: 'In the summer of 1875 Thomas Miller, a policeman, was bathing at Camel's Head with a fellow officer. Neither of them could swim, and Miller was swept away by the current and drowned.' (BO July 1875)

More recently, in September 1892 there was another tragic accident at Camel's Head when a Great Western ballast train, having just passed over the Viaduct, saw its engine leave the track. 'It ran into the bank with such force that is was completely overturned. The engine was smashed almost beyond repair, but the engine driver and the stoker succeeded in getting clear before it ran into the bank. But Henry Pope, guard of the train, who was standing on the engine, was carried with it as it overturned and was buried beneath it.' (WJ 1892)

Above: Two views of what is now the London and South Western railway station at St Budeaux, one looking west from the bridge, the other looking east towards the bridge.
Opposite page: Three views of Camel's Head Creek (Keyham Mill Lake) with the footbridge and Viaduct.

A little further to the north again and we find ourselves in St Budeaux. Like the Three Towns themselves, this is a rapidly growing parish: in 1881 the population was 1,986, and by 1891 it had increased to 2,243, but that figure has since [1898] doubled.

During this period there has been plenty of new development in the area, including around the area now known as St Budeaux Square. Here, in 1895, Joseph Stribling bought land from General John Jago Trelawny for £157, and then having borrowed £4,500, built the Trelawny Hotel, complete with two bars, a bar parlour, club room, coach house and stables with other assorted outbuildings. Stribling died in 1897 and the Octagon Brewery acquired the hotel.

The amount of investment here contrasted starkly with the lack of investment in the recently demolished Millbrook Cottages. Here, in January 1895, died Lydia Prouse, aged 10 months, the infant daughter of James Prouse, a mason's labourer. 'At the inquest into the death, the jury, on going to view the body, found the house in a most ruinous condition, and quite unfit for human habitation. In the same room in which the body was lying was a brother of the deceased, sick of the measles. The window was in some places devoid of glass, exposing the sick child to draughts of a bitterly cold air. No water closet accommodation was attached to the house, neither was there an adequate supply of water.' *(RCG 1895)*

Top left: *Station Square, with the new Co-operative store opened in what had been Stuart House, Trelawny Road in January 1896.* Top right: *The Trelawny Hotel, opened in 1895.* Bottom far left: *The last remnant of Millbrook Cottages in 1899.* Bottom left: *A general view of Millbrook Cottages.* Above middle: *St Budeaux Parish Church.* Above right: *St Budeaux Inn across from the church.*

Despite great advances in its population, St Budeaux still manages to look extremely rural around the church.

Workmen prepare to raise the eastern tube of the Royal Albert Bridge which was opened in 1859.

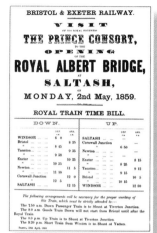

Of all the great structures that have been created in this area during the lifetime of the Queen, few can compare with Brunel's magnificent bridge connecting Devon and Cornwall.

Many felt that such a thing could never be built, including Brunel's father, but great was the joy, when, in the summer of 1857 the first, western, tube and truss section was lifted into place.

'To estimate the numbers that were present is impossible, but at a low computation we should say at least from 30,000 to 40,000.'

Of course, even greater were the celebrations a little under two years later when His Royal Highness Prince Albert, a railway enthusiast, made the six-hour train journey down from Windsor to officiate at the opening of the bridge that had been named in his honour.

Brunel himself was too unwell to attend the event and it wasn't until the end of that summer that he was able to view it from a couch mounted on a flat wagon. The great engineer sadly never recovered and died on 15 September 1859, aged just 53.

Top left: The eastern tube awaits the completion of the supporting pier. Top middle: The entrance to the single track bridge. Top right: An advertisement promoting the opening of the bridge. Bottom: A train makes the crossing.

Above: *The newest Saltash Ferry built by Willoughby Brothers of Millbay in 1892.* Inset: *The third Saltash Ferry, built by the Plymouth Foundry and Engine Works, in 1865, to replace the vessel wrecked earlier that year*

The first steam crossing into Saltash was not the train, it was the ferry, back in 1832. A few years earlier, in 1829, the Earl of Morley, the Saltram-based nobleman who had previously commissioned James Meadows Rendel to provide a floating bridge to cross the Plym, together with Mr A Edgcumbe, Sir William Molesworth and others, obtained an Act of Parliament authorising them to buy the ferry rights from Saltash Corporation. Their steam ferry, again the work of Rendel, was an instant, but not lasting, success and after a year or two it was taken away for renovation and replaced by the old horse-pulled boats that had formerly operated from here.

As it transpired it wasn't until 1850 that the steam service was revived, by which time work had already begun on Brunel's bridge.

Around the same time the Ferry House at Saltash Passage was converted to a coaching house and there can be little doubt that the work on Brunel's masterpiece brought ever-increasing numbers to the area to witness the construction, and even more thereafter to see the finished article for themselves.

Clearly looking to capitalise on the situation, the licensee of the Devonport Inn at the eastern side of the ferry's original path — it was moved when work began on the bridge — decided to rename his premises the Royal Albert Bridge Inn.

On one particular fateful night in 1865 the 'new' steam ferry — she had been built in 1851 — having been moored a little too near the shore, was grounded and slipped into the foreshore mud where she became partially submerged when the tide came in again. Her back was broken in the ensuing endeavours to lift her off and she was damaged beyond repair.

Top: *Fun in the sun at Saltash Passage (Riverside)*. Bottom: *The 1892 Ferry on blocks outside the Ferry House Inn*. Above: *Unloading at Saltash Passage*.

Weston Mill at the head of Weston Mill Lake.

'Leaving Devonport by the Saltash road, we speedily arrive at Weston Mill, a little hamlet deeply seated in a thickly foliaged vale at the head of a creek of the Tamar. Its turnpike house overshadowed by trees — its lichened bridge — its leafy lanes stealing away into haunts of sylvan loveliness — and lofty hills which rise around form an interesting picture of peaceful seclusion, seldom found in the immediate neighbourhood of a populous town. The creek presents an extremely gratifying scene when the tide is up, and is gently rippling round the rock-edged promontories. It then possesses all the charms of a sequestered lake, and is seldom without a rude boat, or perhaps a rustic barge, to add to the general effect.'

So wrote Henry Carrington in his *Excursion from Devonport to Buckland Monachorum*, first published in 1828. In truth the scene is little altered today. The creek of the Tamar at Camel's Head is still properly known as Weston Mill Lake and barges are still being sailed up to unload corn for the mill.

Writing some years after Carrington, GP Hearder noted there was a 'snug little domicile on the immediate right after the bridge had been crossed' where 'as the writer has more than once proved, a nice drop of tea, and, thanks to our favoured county, a basin of cream may at any time be procured for a trifling sum, to assist in wiling away anything but tedious hours.'

Top left: *Ham House, currently in the possession of Dr Trelawny Ross.* Top right: *St Pancras Church.* Right: *Swilly Lodge at the head of Keyam Creek.*

'Tea finished, the pedestrian is invited to descend to the margin of the creek, above a stone arch: here, on a primitive bridge, consisting of a single stone thrown across it, the other bank may be gained; then, having walked about half-way up the hill side, a most pleasant path is discovered, overshadowed by trees, running towards the east, for nearly a quarter of a mile, this walk belongs to the Ham Estate.' Beyond Ham, 'no lover of the picturesque ever thought of passing by Pennycross Chapel without lifting the humble latch of its little gate and straying awhile in its green burial ground.' *(Carrington)*

Among the many interesting properties we find a little to the north of the Three Towns is the imposing mansion of the Henn-Gennys family.

'Thought to have been built 300 years ago, Whitleigh Hall stands upon a park-like lawn of some extent with ornamental pleasure grounds and commands one of the finest views in the West of England.' *(Devonshire)*

Another fine residence is the seat of Captain RJ Hall Parlby, a substantial mansion of granite and stone, dating from 1567, pleasantly situated in extensive and well-wooded grounds.

Close by Manadon at the top of the steep hill we find the aptly named Crown Hill, formerly known as Knackersknowle.

A line of forts, forming the eastern defences of Plymouth, runs through the parish extending from Laira Point to Crown Hill Fort, and a large portion of the land adjoining belongs to the War Department.

The recent (1891-92) construction of new military barracks above the crossroads at Crown Hill and the concomitant arrival of troops and businesses to serve the expanding parish has seen the demolition of a number of older properties in the village, including two public houses: the ancient New Inn and Tamar (formerly the First and Last) and these have been replaced by an altogether more substantial edifice retaining the Tamar name.

Another development around this time has seen a new, redbrick police station take its place in the village alongside the Tamar Hotel.

Top: *Whitleigh Hall.* Above: *Manadon House.* Right: *The new Crown Hill Barracks.*

Top: *Tavistock Road running through Crown Hill village.* Above left and middle: *Two views of the recently demolished Tamar Inn, looking south and north.* Above right: *The new Tamar Hotel and Police Station.*

201

The story perhaps with the biggest implications for Plymouth in recent years though happened much further north of the town boundaries than Crown Hill — at Burrator.

Early in 1881 the town had experienced an acute famine, 'occasioned by a fall of snow which overwhelmed the leat carrying Plymouth's water supply' and 'rendered the inhabitants once more dependent on the wells. Water was sold by the barrel, and the stoppage of factories threw hundreds out of employment.'

A reservoir was constructed at Roborough, but it was inadequate and another precipitation, the blizzard of March 1891, prompted fierce debate about how best to tackle the 'gigantic task: In one night the streets of the Three Towns were covered with snow to the depth of several inches, trees were uprooted within the town, houses were un-roofed, and attempts at vehicular traffic were abandoned.'

'In all some 60,000 tons of material were built into the dam, and, as the foundations were excavated to 53 feet below the bed of the river so as to reach solid rock or avoid suspicion of crevice, the height of the structure from the lowest point to the top of the parapet was 145 feet and storage of 650,000,000 gallons was guaranteed.' *(Whitfeld)*

Various proposals were debated and in the end 'it was decided to throw a dam across the picturesque Burrator gorge that should resist the weight of four times the volume of water that the valley was calculated to hold.'

An Act promoting the scheme was fiercely contested but eventually passed, on 10 June 1893.

Top left: *Derriford House.* Top right: *Work begins on Roborough Reservoir, 1885.*
Left: *Burrator House.* Above: *Construction work at Burrator.*

Left: *Construction of Burrator and completion of dam.*
Above: *Inspection of the completed structure prior to filling.*
Right: *Medal struck by the Mayor John Thomas Bond.*

203

Compton Inn, Compton, looking along Priory Road. Inset top: Priory Road looking back towards the Inn. Inset top left: JT Bond. Inset left: The medal struck to commemorate the boundary change that took in Mutley and Compton in 1896.

COMPTON, MANNAMEAD, MUTLEY AND MORE

In 1887 John Thomas Bond set up a legal practice with Percy T Pearce — Bond Pearce — it was also the year that the 33-year-old solicitor entered local politics and started out on what soon proved to be a remarkable career.

The son of a shoemaker, he had gone to Public School, in Cobourg Street, and had secured a position as office boy to local solicitor Eliot Square just a month or so before his twelfth birthday.

Ten years later he became an articled clerk and by the age of 27 had qualified as a solicitor.

Around the same time the unfortunate Eliot Square had been knocked over and killed by a runaway horse cab in Athenaeum Street and the practice was bought by Christopher Bridgman. Bond soon became an equal partner in the firm.

In 1886 Bridgman left the practice to become Clerk to the Borough Magistrates and the following year Bond entered his partnership with Pearce and so began one of the area's leading legal practices. A passionate Liberal, he was elected Councillor for the Sutton Ward, and so began a parallel career that ten years later saw him universally congratulated by the Council in appreciation of his: 'vigorous advocacy of the interest of the borough in relation to the improvement of the water supply of the Corporation, and also for the able and persistent way in which he has worked for improving the condition of the homes of the poor, and providing them with sanitary and comfortable dwellings; and finally, the Council desires to congratulate him on the fact that during his [second] term of office the boundary of the borough, which had for four centuries remained unaltered, has been largely extended ...'

Top left: Compton School, Chapel and Pear Tree Cottages, directly opposite the Inn. Above: Hartley Reservoir created in the 1860s. Top right: Torr House, resdience of Robert Bayly built in 1883. Bottom right and middle: Two views of Compton Village

Above: *Eggbuckland village.* Left: *Eggbuckland Church looking south.*

A little beyond the revised boundary we find the parish and village of Eggbuckland. It is three miles north by east of Plymouth and is in the Plympton St Mary Union, the Parliamentary subdivision of Tavistock.

'The Church, dedicated to St Erasmus, is an ancient building, containing a chancel, nave, north and south aisles, and embattled tower with six bells; in 1864 it was newly roofed, re-floored, and re-seated, and a new north aisle and chancel added, and a reredos constructed.

'The living is a vicarage in the patronage of the Lord Chancellor, and is valued at £8.4s.4d and in 1881 at £512.' *(Eyre 1898)*

The population 20 years ago was 1,131 and in the following ten years that figure was increased by 501. The area continues to grow.

During the Civil War the Royalists were camped in this area and Prince Maurice and his fellow officers were billeted in the substantial mansion that is Widey Court.

Presently this is the residence of Charles Alfred Fox a director of the Devon & Cornwall Bank that his father and uncles established in 1832. Mr Fox is also chairman of Fox, Eliott & Co., and founder of the Crown Hill Convalescent Home that was set up with other members of his family in 1884.

Above left: *Widey Farm, in the hands of Samuel Kivell, dairyman.* Top right: *Cottages in Widey Lane.* Above right: *Widey Court.*

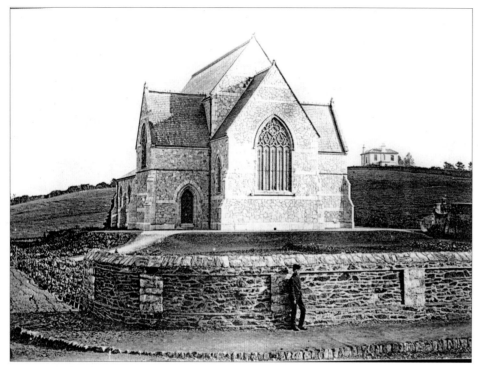

The expansion of Compton Gifford began in earnest in the 1820s when certain prosperous figures from the Three Towns started to look a little further afield for locations in which to build themselves grand villas. At that time Compton had neither church nor chapel and a small edifice was constructed in the heart of the village. However, as more and more substantial properties started to appear to the north of Mutley it became increasingly apparent that a more suitable, and more local, place of worship was needed.

In 1866, the year that the Reverend George Fletcher became curate-in-charge at Compton, a meeting of Mannamead, Compton and other local inhabitants was called by Fletcher and the Reverend Henry Greaves (incumbent at the mother parish of Charles Church), to adopt measures providing the erection of a proposed new church at Mannamead.

A private site was offered by Mrs Betsy Revel and her daughter Elizabeth — Elizabeth's brother, the Reverend Revel, had expressed a wish on his deathbed that something be done for the church.

Accompanying the offer of the land was the request that the church might be named after the Reverend Revel's college at Cambridge — Emmanuel.

Built from the designs of a local architect William Reid, who made no charge for his services, the first corner stone was laid by the Reverend Greaves on 17 June 1869. The initial work was finished by September 1870 and in 1887 a second cornerstone was laid for the building of the transepts, chancel, vestry, and completion of the nave. More recently (1895) a third foundation stone was laid for work on the tower. Originally the intention was to complete the tower with a spire, however funds are, as yet insufficient.

Top: *Emmanuel Church in the 1870s, from Mannamead Road.* Above: *Looking in the opposite direction this is Emmanuel following the second phase of construction work.* Above middle: *The interior following the modifications in 1887.* Right: *The original vision for the church, with a spire.*

The idea for moving out of the heart of the town and into the countryside here is in many respects attributable to the architect who suggested that Plymouth's grand new theatre in 1810 should be located on what was then the outskirts of town, in George Street. Following his own move from London to Plymouth, Mr Foulston lost little time in building himself an impressive dwelling at the bottom of Townsend Hill. Over the next few decades the end of the town was to move inexorably further and further out. In the 1850s Messrs Edward Crispe Ellery, Francis Fowler and John Nicholas Bennett acquired the two fields known as the Mannameads from the Seymour Trustees and before long the two fields had been laid out as a series of splendid villas by Messrs William Damant and the aforementioned William Reid, architects and civil engineers.

Top and middle left: *Looking through the original entrance to Second Avenue, since renamed Seymour Road — the imposing pillars have in recent years been removed (bottom picture).* Top middle: *The road to Eggbuckland from Mannamead Road.* Top right: *Elm Road — note the sign advertising Ashford Estate: Freehold Sites.* Above right: *The Compton tram terminus is a little to the right of this spot, even closer is Emmanuel Church, the road to Compton and Eggbuckland is on the right as are Mr Hender's charming nurseries.*

Across the road from Emmanuel, on the western side of the northern route out of Plymouth to Tavistock, we find a somewhat more recent development in the shape of Thorn Park. A number of substantial properties have been constructed here of late, and in 1893 a formal park was laid out in the middle of the development.

It is said that the park was created as an arboretum and that various eminent naval personnel living in the neighbourhood contributed specimens that they had brought back from all parts of the world.

The park provides a number of delights for the visitor and boasts a rather fine cast-iron, one-man, gentleman's urinal with contemporary decorative panels by Macfarlane's of Glasgow.

The fourth, most westerly side of the park is made up of the boundary wall of Mutley House, long since the residence of the Hawker family. The grounds here also contain a number of interesting trees and shrubs.

Top: Thorn Park Avenue looking towards the gate and lodge of Mutley House. Above: Thorn Park, laid out in 1893.

Top left: *Winter in the grounds of Mutley House.* Middle: *1887, 11-year-old George Poole David Hawker and his 12-year-old brother, Robert Samuel John Norris Hawker, of Mutley House, on their way to Plymouth College through the grounds of Mutley House (right).* Above: *The staff of Mutley House outside the gate and lodge to the grounds.*

Above: *Two views of Thornhill House.* Top right: *1894 advertisement for the Hyde Park Hotel.*

To the west of Mutley House a narrow thoroughfare takes us past Mutley Cottages along Oxford Avenue to Hyde Park Road where we find a modest but quaint and ancient ivy-clad property that once upon a time belonged to Edmund Parker and was, by all accounts, a sometime residence of Sir Francis Drake.

It should be noted that Drake at one time owned over 30 properties in Plymouth and the surrounding area. Curiously enough his leat, bringing water from the Moor, diverted eastwards around this particular property, before crossing the end of Hyde Park Road close by the Hyde Park Hotel.

A three-minute walk from Mutley Station, the Hyde Park sits 'on an elevated and salubrious site, commanding a beautiful view ... there are omnibuses to and from the Town and the Railway Station every ½ hour.' (Wright 1894)

This first-class family hotel (which has a private entrance for families) sits at the bottom of Townsend Hill and it has been in the hands of the Pritchard family for many years now.

Just beyond the Hyde Park stood, until recently, architect John Foulston's late-Georgian Athenian Cottage and indeed a stretch of residences at one time known as Foulston Villas. Here now we find Wilderness Road amongst whose fine houses is the vicarage of Emmanuel Church.

Foulston's Athenian Cottage on Townsend Hill. Mr Foulston, who died in 1841, evidently used to travel the streets in a gig that looked like a Roman chariot.

Left top: *Oxen pull Hugon's Beef Suet van along Mutley Plain.*
Middle: *A horse train outside Mutley Grammar School 1895.*
Bottom: *Mutley Station, opened in 1871, six years before North Road, Ermington Terrace running behind it.*

'Mutley Plain is now a favourite promenade, but year after year it decreases in attractiveness as the town spreads out on every hand, and the country is further off than ever.' (W 1878)

Meanwhile, reminiscing about life back in the 1850s, Benjamin Densham, an old boy of Mannamead School recalled that 'On the east side of Mutley Plain were no houses whatever. It was bordered by a very old hedge, low on the road side, but deep down to the level of the field, along which ran a rope-walk. The view to the Laira and Saltram was considered very fine; indeed the walk along Mutley Plain was one of the prettiest in the Town and neighbourhood.'

Of course, in those days, he added, 'there were practically no houses between Alton Terrace, North Hill and Knackersknowle [Crown Hill], except those in Mannamead Avenue and Seymour Road.'

It is all very different now. Mutley Baptist Chapel was built in 1868 from designs by Messrs Ambrose & Snell, at a cost of nearly £8,000, while on the other side of the Plain, a little further north, Mutley Methodist was opened on 12 October 1881.

'This, the most beautiful building the Wesleyans of Plymouth possess,' was also the work of HJ Snell. 'Mr Snell has designed a great many chapels in and around Plymouth of late years and this is one of his masterpieces, if not his chef d'oeuvre.' (WMN 1881)

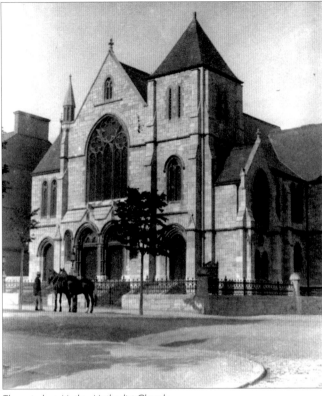

The spireless Mutley Methodist Church.

'The Mutley Railway Station is below in the valley, the railway passing under the Plain by a short tunnel at this point.

'On every side new terraces and villas are springing into existence, so that in a very short space of time the fields will be no longer visible.' (W 1878)

It was indeed to be a short space of time, today Mutley Plain is a thriving commercial centre.

On the last day of December 1889 the Plymouth Co-operative Society bought ground there, 'building thereon two of the best and most handsome and commodious shops to be seen in the neighbourhood, carrying on there a Grocery, Butchery, Dairy and Boot Department.'

Others swiftly followed in their wake.

There were not a great many businesses here before the arrival of the Co-op, one of them however was the eminently successful enterprise of Mr CJ Park, the Chemist. Mr Charles Park took on the brand new pharmacy that had opened in 1864 at No.1 Mutley Plain in 1885 and has recently (1897) moved the operation to No.12.

Another business to open here in the 1860s was John Dickenson's Fortescue Hotel which at that time was just inside the Plymouth boundary — the line then was marked by the railway line west of the Plain, the pavement on its western side and the lane above what is now Connaught Avenue.

Top: *Two views of Park's Pharmacy, with Mr Park, and staff.* Above: *North along Mutley Plain towards the Hyde Park Hotel — note Mutley Methodist now has its spire.*

Meanwhile another development on the western side of the Plain, saw the establishment of Plymouth College (Plymouth High School for Boys prior to 1883) in 1877. The first three years of its existence were spent in Erme House, at the top of Ermington Terrace.

'Nearby was a blacksmith's forge at the open door of which boys going home from school would stop to look in and see the shoeing of horses, the mounts perhaps of some of the six to eight of their school fellows who used to start off in a cavalcade of ponies along Mutley Plain to reach home on the outside borders of the town.

'Regular public road transport hardly existed. Mutley was close to fields and country roads ... Masters were accustomed to walk to school in cap and gown, even I think from so far off as Hill Park Crescent.' So recalls one of the first pupils at the school, Charles Serpell, who joined as a nine-year-old in 1879.

The first headmaster was George Bennett, a Cambridge graduate who had previously been the headmaster of an important Preparatory School in Rugby: 'Boys responded to his evident liking for the work they, and he, were doing ... He read us Erchmann-Chatrian's "Waterloo," and rode a classroom chair into battle against a British square ... His French was good and his enthusiasm a fine stimulus to appreciation of a great story.'

In 1880 the school was moved, mid-term, into the as yet incomplete building at Ford Park.

Top left: *Plymouth College main building - note the unfinished wall on the right.*
Bottom: *Lower corridor in 1896.* Right: *The first school photograph at Ford Park, in 1880.*

'Prayers,' recalls Serpell, 'were read in the lower corridor, the Headmaster standing at the top of the lowest flight of stairs from which his eye commanded the school drawn up before him.'

It wasn't long before the school had reached its present form, but that is still, as far as the founding fathers are concerned, not the complete development, and plans for additional buildings, including a chapel and principal entrance, as drawn up by architects Paull & Sonella, are still the aspiration of the Governing Body.

Nevertheless the school has thrived and in 1896 it merged with the slightly older — and at one time very influential — neighbour Mannamead School. The latter having been set up by the former head of Plymouth's Grammar School, the Reverend Peter Holmes, in Wellington Villa, of Seymour Road, in 1854.

The celebrated author, Eden Philpott, who has had many novels published in the 1890s, was an early pupil there, and his work contains plenty of local references, most notably to his beloved Dartmoor.

Plymouth College plays a number of sports (Cricket, Association Football, Fives, Athletics ...) and a few of its old boys were instrumental in setting up Argyle Athletic in 1886, they also provided Argyle with regular fixtures in those early days.

'We hesitated between the Rugby and Association game,' recalled another former pupil a few years ago, 'a serious accident which happened whilst we were playing the former, decided us in favour of the latter.'

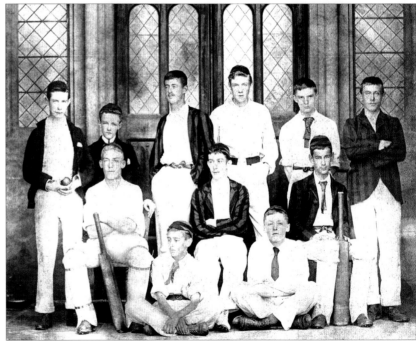

Above: Section of the Plymouth College Cadet Corps in front of the school 1897. Top right: Plymouth College Association Football team 1883-4. Bottom right: 1894 Cricket team: Back l-r: PL Coleridge, GGH Reade, HH Butcher, RJP Thomas, HC Paige, RHS More. Middle: AWS Brock, G Tucker, HA Brown. Front AJ Ellis, DH Magnus

Established a few years earlier than the boy's school, and just a little closer to town, was Plymouth High School for Girls.

Opened in 1874, like Plymouth College it spent a few years in a temporary home, Sherwell House, before relocating to the purpose-built edifice erected within the grounds of a Jacobean dwelling known as North Hill (which became the headmistress' house) in 1877. Miss Annie Kendal was the school's first head — she has since left to set up a new school, Plymouth College for Girls, in Lockyer Street.

From the top of North Hill fine views are to be had over the Houndiscombe valley towards the bottom of which we find the burial ground established by the Plymouth, Stonehouse and Devonport Cemetery Company in 1846. It is very pleasantly situated, and the ground is well enclosed. The first interment was made in December, 1848, since which time field after field has been added, until the place has become a veritable 'city of the dead.'

Top: *Plymouth High School for Girls* Above: *The Plymouth, Devonport and Stonehouse Cemetery.*

'There are two chapels in the cemetery, one for the Church portion, and the other for the Dissenters, and a special burial ground for the Jews. The grounds contain some interesting monuments.'

The original Houndiscombe Estate was bounded by North Road, Ford Park and Mutley Plain and ran down as far as Pennycomequick where once stood Houndescombebrigge. The bridge traversed the two streams running down from Torr and Houndiscome.

The Derry family acquired the estate from the Sherwills earlier this century and they, in turn, had taken possession of it some two hundred years before that. The estate is currently the property of the Rev Thomas Bewes. The area around Houndiscombe has, of late, been much developed, Houndiscombe House remains, at present, an obstacle to future development, as does the farm itself. It is interesting to recount that near the site of the house there was a defensive post known as the Little Pennycomequick Work constructed during the Civil War.

This page: Two views of Houndiscombe Farm with and without snow, note the two small spires of the cemetery chapels above the farm on the skyline — the farm incidentally was demolished in 1902, soon after it had been gutted by fire, while the House would be taken down in 1904.

Beyond the Cemetery gates 'we proceed by the Cemetery Road towards Pennycomequick, passing on the way the now desolate Devonport Borough Prison. The future of this large building is still uncertain. It was at one time thought that the Lords of the Admiralty would enlarge it, and use it as a Naval Prison.' (W 1878)

Built in 1849 at a cost of about £12,500 to the designs of Messrs. Fuller & Gingell, it was one of 54 convict prisons to have been erected in the 1840s in the wake of the end of the transportation of criminals to Australia. Another institution, Plymouth Prison, just off the top of Greenbank Hill — 'erected without the precincts of the town' — was completed a few months earlier. All were constructed to the same plan as Pentonville — the model prison — which was completed in 1842.

A large three-winged affair, it contained cells for 66 prisoners, male and female, a chapel, surgery, baths, convalescent rooms and the necessary offices and apartments. The prison also contained four cells for solitary confinement, 'arranged for the admission of air, but not of light, and twenty four separate airing grounds to accommodate one prisoner each, rotating from a centre in which an officer is placed.'

In 1877 another Prison Act introduced national centralisation, 113 prisons were taken over and 38 were closed, including this one.

Four years after Wright's speculation detailed above, the prison was sold to John Martin of Martin and Son, the large Devonport firm of builders and contractors and by 1882 the prison had been razed.

Wake Street was immediately constructed on part of the site and Holdsworth Street followed soon afterwards. The gatehouse, built to house the governors and porters, was retained and converted as domestic accommodation.

'Our course now lies to the east, the road west leads to Milehouse and the Saltash Road, that in front to Stoke, Devonport and Morice Town. At the angle of the road will be noticed the well-kept nursery grounds of Mr Joel Roberts, above which stands the newly erected North Road Passenger Station, in the joint use of GWR and L&SWR. It is spacious and well designed for extensive traffic and is gradually gaining public favour. It is indeed a great convenience to the inhabitants of the northern part of the town. The GW trains pass from hence into Millbay Station, the L&SW across the loop-line bridge into their new station at Devonport, running for a short distance over the Cornish line.' (ibid)

Top: Devonport Prison at Pennycomequick - opened in 1849, closed 1877. Above: General view of Pennycomequick. Inset: The Pennycomequick toll house.

Following the line of the Great Western Railway westwards out of North Road and walking across the top of the tunnel at Mutley, we emerge on the eastern side of Mutley Plain and another area where green fields are rapidly being swallowed up by development.

Construction work has, since the 1870s, been moving east along Alexandra Road.

Until very recently there was green space either side of the railway until reaching the bottom of Elm Lane and approaching the bridge under the track with Lipson Farm on the northern side and Lipson House on the southern side.

Opposite this vantage point, Lipson Hill, which until the construction of the Embankment at the beginning of the Nineteenth Century had been the principal eastern route out of town.

On our right as we come out from under the bridge we see the brand new, redbrick buildings of the Bedford Brewery.

Established, as the name suggests, in Bedford Street back in 1824, the business, which started out primarily as Polkinghorne & Company, boomed and after a good 50 years there was a complete reconstruction of their premises there. It was this redevelopment that led them to promote the Bedford Brewery name above the original brand.

Clearly, however, that expansion was ultimately insufficient to cope with the present level of interest in their popular beers. Thus it was in 1898 that they moved out to Alexandra Road and a site that almost backed on to the newly created Lipson Vale Halt (doubtless a factor in their decision to move).

Now it was even easier to move their barrels around the county and indeed country, in addition to the two dozen or so pubs that the brewery control in the local area.

The pale ale, mild and porter (so called because it was originally made for porters) are particularly popular as is their Superior Brown Stout which, for many years now, has been available at one shilling and fourpence a gallon.

As we reach the bottom of the valley, before making our way up the steep slope of Lipson Hill, it is worth reflecting on the fact that it wasn't that long ago, in the overall scheme of such things, that waters of Lipson Creek reached up this far.

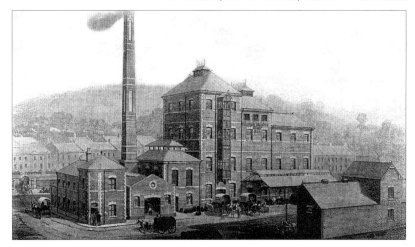

Top: Bedford Brewery 1898, from Lipson Halt. Above right: Looking across to Lipson Hill. Bottom right: The entrance to Lipson House at the end of Alexandra Road.

At the top of Lipson Hill, and running from Lipson Road to Beaumont Road, is Seymour Avenue West. Many of the houses here enjoy a pleasant view of the recently extended Freedom Fields Park.

The name commemorates the annual celebrations of the last of the Breton Raids almost 500 years ago, celebrations that formerly took place nearer the old town. More famously and more recently another battle was fought in this area, in December 1643.

This was the Sabbath Day fight of the Civil War and it marked the closest point that the Royalist forces got to the town.

A few years ago, in 1891, a memorial to this bloody encounter in which many lives were lost, was erected at the top of the park, in front of the impressive terrace that commands spectacular seaward views — Queen's Gate. We will now walk through the park and head for top of Greenbank Road.

Top left: *Looking down Lipson Hill.* Top right: *One of Walter Hender's two Chemists in the area, this one is in Seymour Avenue, the other in Tothill Road.*
Bottom left: *Freedom Fields Park with the new Sabbath Day memorial in front of Queen's Gate.* Above right: *Looking down Seymour Avenue with the Park on the right.*

Plymouth's first proper general public hospital — the South Devon and East Cornwall Hospital — was opened on the corner of Sussex Street and Notte Street in 1840 and although it expanded over the years it never sported more than 75 beds across eight wards, but it was rapidly rendered inadequate and in 1877 it was resolved to build a new hospital on a site on the outskirts of town, in Speccotts Fields on the northern reaches of the Seven Trees Estate at Greenbank.

London architects Coe & Robinson were invited to draw up plans and on Friday 29 July 1881 the Earl of Mount Edgcumbe laid the foundation stone for a new South Devon and East Cornwall Hospital. A little over three years later, in September 1884, the new facility was ready to open. A crowd of more than 7,000 people turned up on the Saturday before the premises was put into service.

'A good portion of the visitors were more or less from the working classes' ... which is good, 'seeing that the hospital is an institution directly for their benefit.'

The whole project was made possible largely thanks to two great local families, the Edgcumbes and the Lopes. Sir Massey Lopes, like his father before him, had been connected with the earlier Sussex Place hospital and became President of the New Hospital in Greenbank Road. The Lopes and Maristow wards were constructed mainly through his contributions in 1884. The Chapel was built by him in 1895 and endowed with £2,000. In the last eight or nine years Sir Massey has endowed the facility with a further £14,000.

To put these benefactions in context, the entire cost of construction of the original development was just £32,000.

The South Devon and East Cornwall Hospital at the top of Greenbank Road.

Main picture: *The Church of St Jude, in Tothill Lane, built from the designs of Mr Hine and consecrated in 1876, the Rev. Bewes liberally subscribed to the building fund.*
Inset top: *Beaumont Park.* Inset bottom: *Tothill House, formerly a Culme Seymour property and pulled down in 1890, it stood a little beyond Beaumont House.*

Continuing our ramble down Greenbank Road we arrive at another relatively new development, Tothill Avenue (1882), along the western side of which we find one of the town's newest recreation grounds — Beaumont Park. Beaumont had been the residence of the Reverend Thomas Archer Bewes, a lifelong bachelor whose wish it was for his estate to be sold to the town for that very purpose.

The Reverend Bewes died in 1892 and just a year or two ago Beaumont House opened as a temporary Museum for the town.

Opened to the public free of charge on Sundays in 1899 'the working classes forthwith attended in large numbers to view the pictures and curiosities.'

It is worth noting that this area has, of late, become much more accessible, with the tram route that was laid out along the newly developed Beaumont Road in 1896 — a route that has became Plymouth's first electrified stretch of tramline in 1899, and, of course, the railway terminus at Friary that came into service in 1879.

Top: *Laira House, formerly residence of Fanny Julian and, since 1882, serving as Plymouth School Board's Truant Industrial School, where persistent truants are kept for 72 days at a time.* Main picture: *Lipson Vale at the dawn of the Twentieth Century.*

Left: top: *Plymbridge.* Middle: *Colebrook, with the Methodist church on the left.*
Bottom: *Colebrook, same view looking in the opposite direction.*
Right: top: *Boringdon Hall.* Middle: *Earl's Mill factory.* Bottom: *Plympton Station.*

PLYMPTON: ST MARY AND ST MAURICE

The first train station to open in the wider Plymouth neighbourhood was at Plympton (Colebrook), and on 5 May 1848, when Daniel Gooch drove the Pisces, an engine of his own design, into this part of the world for the first time, tens of thousands of people from the Three Towns turned out to witness the spectacle.

Interestingly enough, the population of Plympton has not appeared to grow off the back of this revolution in transport to quite the extent that some of her neighbours have: indeed the population of Plympton St Mary, which includes the villages of Ridgway, Underwood, Colebrook, Hemerdon, Sparkwell, Venton and Lee Mill, while undoubtedly being an extensive parish, has witnessed a slight drop in numbers in recent years — from 3,513 in 1881 to 3,471 in 1891. The parish church, built in the Decorated and Perpendicular styles, is dedicated to St Mary.

The church is a spacious and handsome edifice, consisting of chancel, north and south porches, a fine tower, containing eight bells, a spacious nave, with two side aisles and two exterior aisles, which were anciently chapels.

The living is a vicarage valued at £300 and the vicarage itself, erected at Colebrook, stands on an eminence and commands a fine view of the surrounding country.

It is believed that St Mary's was consecrated in 1311, almost 200 years after the Priory at Plympton had been founded by Bishop Warwist, a nephew of William the Conqueror.

Dating from those days and before are the Pathfields, part of an ancient trackway running down Plympton Hill, through Longbrook Street, Sugar Lane along the west side of the parish church of Plympton Erle — St Maurice.

Left: *St Mary's Church.* Right: *The Plympton Pathfields, lime trees were planted on the borders of the path to commemorate the Queen's Jubilee in 1897.*

Plympton St Maurice, like St Mary, is of ancient foundation and includes a portion of the village of Ridgway.

A market town pleasantly situated in a fertile vale it sits two miles east of the River Plym and is five miles east by north of Plymouth.

The population here is somewhat less than Plympton St Mary and it too has declined of late, rather than grown, albeit in no great measure. In 1881 the population was 1,146 and that number had fallen by seven at the time of the last census in 1891.

'The parish church of St Maurice is a handsome stone structure containing nave, aisles and tower and was thoroughly renovated, and a new organ built, in 1878.

'The living is a rectory, in the patronage of the Dean and Canons of Windsor, and is valued at £140.

'The grammar school, erected in 1664, and repaired in 1868, is a fine building in the Perpendicular style.

'Plympton House, the former seat of the Treby family, is a handsome mansion with tasteful grounds, now used as a lunatic asylum, having accommodation for about 60 patients.

'There is a public hall, situated in the village, used for concerts and other entertainments. The first Monday in each month is the market day, which is only for cattle.

'The Earl of Morley is Lord of the Manor.' (E 1898)

Left top and bottom: *Two views of the Ridgway, Plympton.* Top right: *The George Hotel.*

Following the passing of the Reform Act in 1832 Plympton lost its Parliamentary representation and with it some of the prestige and important financial patronage ebbed away from the Mayor and his Council.

Over the next few decades the Court of Alderman and the Common Council witnessed a further erosion of their influence and by 1860 a position had been reached whereby it was decided that 'the interests of the inhabitants would be best consulted by suspending operations of the charter, by refraining from the election of a Chief Magistrate.'

And so from that year to this no Mayor has been elected for Plympton and two years later the old court, cells and other rooms were removed from the Guildhall in Fore Street and a new hall capable of seating 300 people took its place.

The impact on the population has already been alluded to and whereas the Plymouth population has increased sixfold over the last hundred years, in Plympton it has not even doubled over the same time period.

Top left: *Fore Street, St Maurice.* Above: *Three views of Underwood showing the Union Inn and Ye Olde Ring of Bells.*

St Mary and All Saints, Plymstock.

PLYMSTOCK, HOOE AND WEMBURY

Left: *Turnchapel and Oreston Steam Ferry.* Right: *View from Saltram.*

'With the villages of Oreston, Turnchapel, Hooe, Elburton, Pomphlett, Billacombe and Staddiscombe, Plymstock is a parish and a large straggling village, situated in a pleasant valley, near Cattewater Harbour and Plymouth Sound, three miles east by south of Plymouth. 'The church, dedicated to St Mary and All Saints is a large edifice, in the Perpendicular style, with a tower containing six bells.

'In 1886 it was re-roofed, re-seated, a new vestry added, and several other improvements effected, costing £2,500. The fifteenth-century rood screen was restored in 1877.

'The nearest railway here is a station on a branch of the London & South Western Railway from Plymouth, now carried on to Turnchapel; other near stations are at Marsh Mills and Plympton. Steam ferries run every half-hour from Oreston to Phoenix Wharf. (*E 1898*)

Like Plympton, a little further up the Plym, the population here has not experienced the boom conditions seen on the other side of the river and between 1881 and 1891 it too fell — from 3,174 to 3,102.

The Duke of Bedford is the Lord of the Manor and indeed the Manor has been in the hands of that family for centuries. In more recent times the seventh and eighth Dukes have either sold or gifted land here for different purposes, most notably for a variety of church buildings both in Plymstock itself. The current Duke, Herbrand Russell, is the second son of the ninth Duke.

'Agreeable hours are to be mildly dissipated on the banks of the Plym — the river that once encircled Plymouth. Boat or steamer from the Barbican, and also South Western train, will transport the visitor to Plymstock — a village of striking rural characteristics and of historic consequence as the scene of the siege of Mount Stamford by the forces of Charles.

'Parties will appreciate the pastoral delights of the woods at Saltram — the noble seat of the Earl of Morley. In the park the rhododendrons flourish in such glorious clusters that visitors are admitted only on the condition that they leave their baskets at home, so irresistible has proved the temptation to replace the edibles with blooms. The mansion contains a fine collection of the works of Reynolds, but the gallery is no less representative of other masters. Alternatively, a delicious ramble is afforded in Radford Woods, which ascend from the same bank of the river. Landing at the little village of Hooe, at the head of the creek which winds at this point, the visitor will soon enjoy the shelter of the glades.' (*PaaHC 1900*)

'Hooe is a separate ecclesiastical parish, taken out of Plymstock in 1855, and comprises the villages of Hooe, Turnchapel, Batten, Bovisand and Staddon, and has a population of 1,364, including 400 soldiers, stationed at Staddon, Bovisand and Stamford forts.' (E 1898) The forts were constructed in the 1860s as part of the defensive ring around the Three Towns.

'Consecrated in 1855, the church is dedicated to St John, and consists of a nave, chancel and south aisle and holds about 400 worshippers. There is a large National School adjoining the church. The church was designed by Cornish architect WH White and is based largely on a fourteenth-century plan although the form of the school house and school are more contemporary.' (ibid)

At the head of Hooe Lake we find one of the oldest properties in the area the ancient Hooe Barn. Meanwhile at the head of Radford Lake sits the largest property in the Plymstock area, Radford House. In the hands of the Harris family for hundreds of years, the Harris's are principal stakeholders in the Naval Bank established by Messrs Harris, Harris, Turner & Herbert in 1773.

Top left: *Radford Castle* Top right: *Radford Boat House.* Above left: *Hooe Lake 1892.* Above right: *Hooe Barn 1892.*

There is little doubt that the construction of the Iron Bridge across the Plym in 1827 did much to improve the commercial opportunities in the South Hams with regard to the opening up of market places in the Three Towns, however it is anticipated that the prospects created by the arrival of the 'Iron Horse' on this side of the Plym will do wonders for those places now accessible via rail, notably for the last outpost on the new line — Turnchapel.

Friday 1 January 1897 was the red-letter day for Turnchapel as this was the day that passenger services commenced in and out of this bustling hamlet on the banks of the Cattewater.

Although there is no shortage of watermen to make the crossing into Sutton Harbour, and there is also a regular ferry service, the availability of an easy land-based route in and out of the area will, it is hoped, be a boon to those catering for day trippers.

Turnchapel with the Boringdon Arms in the middle distance on the left.

While Turnchapel undoubtedly benefits from the to-ing and fro-ing of many temporary visitors — which is why the Oreston and Turnchapel Steamboat Company invested in a new pier for their steam ferries in 1889 — the greater attractions lie beyond this point, at Mount Batten, Bovisand and beyond.

Some years earlier, in 1881, the company had secured landing rights at Mount Batten, and on a rare bank holiday many thousands make the trip across to wander around the headland.

Rough and rugged, this is, as yet, a largely unspoilt section of coastline and many vessels have come to grief here, indeed of more than 250 craft that have been wrecked in and around Plymouth Sound in the last hundred years, over 30 have been lost in and around Batten Bay, a third of them on the reef itself, although the number has fallen greatly since the pier was constructed out over the Batten Reef in 1883.

Top left: *The new (1889) pier at Turnchapel.* Middle left: *A view of the seventeenth century tower.* Bottom left and above: *George Hine's Castle Inn.* Top right: *Day trippers.*

Top: *View across Mount Batten to the Royal Citadel (contemporary with Batten Tower) and Plymouth in the distance. In the foreground we see Johan II a brig wrecked off the Batten Reef in 1865.* Right: *A lone tug guides a sailing ship out to the Sound.*

If Mount Batten may fairly be described as sparsely populated then what adjective might we use for the stretch of coastline beyond it? Prior to the present century we can find little or no trace of a name to refer to the that stretch of land between Mount Batten and Staddon, a stretch we now know as Jennycliff.

Curiously enough the earliest versions of that name appear to break the epithet into two, as in Jenny Cliff, leading us to wonder whether this, like Staddon itself has an animal based derivation. Staddon, like all others in Devon, and there are several, is a combination of two words, 'stott' or 'stod' and 'dun.'

The former is our 'stud' or 'bullock' while the latter signifies a 'hill', so Staddon is the 'hill of the bullocks.' Is then Jenny Cliff a cliff of the donkeys? Jenny is used in reference to the female of a number of species, and since the beginning of this century that has come to include the humble ass.

Jennycliff Beach, a popular resort for day trippers.

If we continue our coastline ramble yet further we come to our next most populous parish, that of Wembury. An extensive manor, currently in the hands of Richard Cory, JP, who resides in Langdon Court. The 2,000-acre estate includes most of Wembury, Down Thomas and Knighton.

The parish church, dedicated to St Werburgh, sits high above Wembury Mill overlooking the entrance to Plymouth Sound and the dramatic, and now uninhabited island known as the Mewstone. Local legend suggests that when Victoria came to the throne the island was inhabited and had its own public house.

Views of Wembury Church with Wembury Mill evident in the foreground of the main photograph.

237

Looking across to Cattedown, an industrial community with a number of shops and public houses, among them the ancient Passage House Inn and the Three Crowns.

CATTEDOWN AND CATTEWATER

While we have been happily discussing what the tourist can see around the Three Towns it is perhaps worth a mention of what recently so nearly came to pass and which, if it had, would have brought many more tourists in its wake.

'At the instance of the Chamber of Commerce, opinion was sought as to the possibility of converting Cattewater into a harbour adapted to the development of commerce and the necessities of ocean liners.

'Explorations of the bed conducted by Sir Wolfe Barry and Mr Bretherton disclosed a deposit capable of being removed to any depth required, and the solitary obstacle to navigation of a substantial kind was "a patch of rock" whose removal presented no engineering difficulties.

'As part of the foreshore had been acquired by the Corporation, the cost of obtaining the remainder, constructing the necessary wharves and docks, and lengthening the Batten Breakwater, was estimated at £660,000.

'When the scheme was first unfolded by Mr JT Bond, the Mayor, it was welcomed with patriotic fervour, and Sir Wolfe Barry's eulogy of the Cattewater — Catwater had ceased to be the form of spelling — as possessing unrivalled capacity was accepted as sufficient basis for hoping that Plymouth would yet develop the finest natural harbour in the world. The Council was so enamoured by the prospect that only one member voted against the resolution, and the approval of the ratepayers was tempestuously accorded at the Guildhall meeting.'

Such is not to say that there was no opposition, but 'after a polemical warfare of unprecedented virulence, which extended over several weeks, the town was polled, and the numbers recorded for the proposed Bill were 8,778 and 5,933 against.'

However a 'veto was imposed by the Lords of the Admiralty, who, claiming Plymouth as a naval port, blocked the scheme on the ground that ocean liners would too largely draw upon the two deep water channels that admit of entrance to the Sound.'

Left: The Passage House Inn. Right: Cattedown and the Cattewater from Mount Batten, writing in 1894 in his excellent Dictionary of Fable and Phrase suggested that Cattewater is a 'corruption of chateau (chat-eau); as the castle at the mouth of the Plym used to be called,' an attractive notion not hitherto advanced in any of our published histories!

Above: Laira and the Embankment.
Left: Prince Rock, Plymouth Electricity Works, opened on 22 September 1899 by the Mayor, Alderman John Pethick, whose company also executed the building work. The foundation stone had been laid on 21 April the previous year by the then Mayor JT Bond.

ELECTRICITY WORKS, PLYMOUTH

'"Nothing succeeds like success," and certainly Plymouth may congratulate itself upon the success of the inauguration of its municipal electricity undertaking. Everything went off admirably yesterday.'

'The tramcars ran smoothly and with punctuality, and the passengers, as well as the crowds of curious and admiring spectators who lined the road, were evidently more than satisfied with the experiment.

'As to the lighting of the streets, there is not a fault to be found. The arc lamps are sufficiently close together, and there is not likely to be serious complaint of the "spottiness" which is frequently alleged as an objection to this form of lighting.

'The effect will be better judged on a dark night, when there is no moon, but even on the darkest night it will no doubt be found that the general appearance of the streets under the new form of lighting is admirable.

'One of the best achievements of the Electricity Committee and their engineer is in the improved lighting of the Hoe. This fine promenade is now so well lighted that it ought to become as favourite a resort after nightfall as it has always been in the daylight.

'It is a pity that the crowds of summer visitors could not have had the benefit of this during the last few months of fine weather, but it will be there for them next year, and will certainly be a great addition to the attractions of Plymouth.

'Mr Rider said yesterday that the cost of electric arc lighting is double that of the gas it displaces. As a matter of fact, according to his own report in July 1896 the cost is two and a half times as much. In other words, the arc lamps now expected will cost £1,184 per annum, as against £475 paid for the gas lamps put out of use. With a rate of 7 shilling in the pound we must, therefore, be content with a moderate use of electric arc lighting.

'For the centre of the town and the Hoe it is a fitting luxury, but other parts of the borough must do without it, unless the rates are to be still further increased.

'Incandescent gas lighting is brightening up some of the main thoroughfares in which the electric cables have not been laid, and as this is much cheaper than electric lighting and promises to be practically as effective, the ratepayers will, no doubt, be satisfied with it for the present, if not for all time.

'In Liverpool the streets are lit by incandescent gas lamps, although the Corporation own the electric lighting plant, while the gasworks are in the hands of a company who do not sell gas at 1s 9d per 1,000 feet.

John Rider: Appointed Borough Electrical Engineer 1898

'With reference to the tramcars, the one thing now to hope for is that the new system of traction may be speedily applied to the Compton section. It ought not to take up anything like as long a time as the fitting up of the Prince Rock line. Progress will necessarily be affected by the works for the widening of Tavistock Road, but everybody willl welcome the day when the painful spectacle of horses toiling up the steep hills to Mannamead, with heavily laden tramcars is no longer to be witnessed.

'We do not share the admiration of Mr Rider for the overhead system, for whatever may be said of it, it is certainly not pretty. Still, it is effective in operation, and as it is apparently the only system commercially possible, it is better that we should have this than continue the system of horse traction, with it still more objectionable features.' (WMN 23 September 1899)

Top feft: *Beechwood Cottage.* Middle: *Milton's Temple.* Top right: *The Folly.* Above: *Cremyll Point and HMS* Impregnable.

MOUNT EDGCUMBE

'"Tis not prejudice that prompts the lay when Mount Edgcumbe is the theme." Thus discoursed Carrington of the wave-washed home of the Edgcumbes — its floral graces and wooded charms, where the exotic bloom as in a perpetual springtime, and the trees that fringe the coastline droop their boughs and kiss the surf.

'The mansion is Elizabethan, consecrated by many an act of devotion to the throne of England, and of good repute for hospitalities to august visitors — kings, queens and emperors, princes and princesses of all nationalities.

'The house is rarely open to the inspection of the public, but the park, with its labyrinthine walks and elegant terraces, leading to Milton's Temple, the Cottage, the Rotunda or the Amphitheatre, with acclivities displaying in luxuriance the cedar of Libanus, the polar of Carolina, huge planes and foreign tulip trees, commanding oaks and spreading chestnuts, is readily available.

'The zig-zag walks will bring the visitor now to Picklecombe, with its pastoral valley; again, to the groves where the deer browse without dread of the rifle; then to the ruins of the old Stonehouse gates, re-erected here to suggest the survival of an ancient tower; and away to Reading Point, an elevation from which the length of the Breakwater may be commanded.

'Here the panorama of the Sound spreads as in a map — rich in colour, bright with sails and animate with wreathing smoke.

'If after this feast of views, the tourist is favoured to enter the English, French and Italian gardens, with their fantastic fountains and marble statuaries, festooned bowers and fruiting orangeries, imposing magnolias and embowered retreats, his happiness should be perfect.

'Barnpool with its delicate lights and shades, must not be overlooked, for many a sheltered cave is there, hidden between the weather-beaten rocks, the shore lapped by water clear as crystal and the daydream of the bather.'(PaaHC 1900)

From top: *Cremyll landing stage: View of Cremyll Point. Mount edgcumbe House.*
Left: *Picklecombe Fort.*

Watching work on the farm.

RURAL LIFE

While there are but a few farms left within the boundaries of the Three Towns today, a journey around the villages that border Plymouth, Stonehouse and Devonport, will show us that farming and market gardens are still the principal primary source of employment in these areas. These trades also support a number of other key professions in each of these areas — the carpenter, the wheelwright and the blacksmith among them.

In Eggbuckland alone, in addition to several thriving market gardeners we find: John Barltess at Lees Farm; Henry Blake at Thornbury; Benjamin Butland, Leigham; James Crews, Higher Efford; Robert Cundy, Fancy Farm; John Doidge, Mainstone; William Doidge, Little Efford; James Down, Goose Well; Francis Gloyn, Deer Park; Peter Hannaford, Coleridge Farm; Henry Hannaford, Bircham Farm; Samuel Hensleigh, Crown Hill; Samuel Kivell, Widey Farm; Mrs Emma Knapman, Berries Farm; George Moses, Egg Buckland; William Parsons, market gardener and dairyman at Doidge's farm; Mrs Edith Perry, Cressbrook Farm; Joseph Robins, Crown Hill; William Rowe, Frogmore Farm; John Rowland, Derriford Farm; Robert White, Bowden Farm.

Notwithstanding some poor harvests in the 1880s, the farming community is still prospering although the numbers employed are not as great as they were at the beginning of Queen Victoria's reign.

At that time it was estimated that around one in four of the population of the country worked in the countryside.

In the last decade or so the ability to ship frozen meat into the country from Australia, New Zealand and South America has had a noticeable impact on British farming generally, as, indeed, has the importing of cereal from North America.

Farming scenes from around the Three Towns.

Top left: *Two new borns.* Middle: *Toddler with pram.* Top right: *Girls with dollies and boy with hoop (four of the seven main toy dealers, incidentally, are in Union Street — Gaylards and Dabbs — and Pembroke Street — Kirk's and Charles Witts).* Bottom left: *Girl with pram.* Middle: *Girl with a bicycle (these have become very fashionable since the 1880s).* Right: *Two boys with guns, and a lad with a cigarette and dog.*

CHILDHOOD

One group of people for whom life has improved over the last 60 years or so has been the young. In recent years there have been very positive indications that the rate of infant mortality is falling — it has been between 15-20% for most of the present century, suggesting that almost one in five children are taken from us before reaching their fifth birthday. Measles, scarlet fever, whooping cough and diarrhoea are the principal offenders.

The passing of the Education Act in 1870 for the first time has forced local authorities to provide schools for children between the ages of five and twelve, a move that was made mandatory for both boys and girls ten years later. In 1891 there was a widening of the net to include children of all classes as the school pence fee was abolished and primary education became free for all.

'More recently the age for compulsory school attendances has ben raised from 11 to 12, exceptions being made under certain conditions in the case of children employed in agriculture.

'A child can learn comparatively little which will be of service in the after life before the age of 12, yet out of the 5,600,000 children on the school registers less than 763,000 are over 12 years of age.

'In Plymouth large areas have recently been covered by new houses and the deficiency is of uncertain and increasing amount. Probably between 2,000 and 3,000 fresh places are needed almost at once. 'The School Board are alive to the need and suitable provision is being made. At St Budeaux and Pennycross school accommodation is deficient, but there will be no difficulty in providing the needed accommodation.

'Bad attendance is very prevalent, and over 20,000 children are daily absent in Devon alone. In Devon 80.87 per cent of regularity of attendances is secured, whilst in Cornwall only 77.28 per cent is obtained. Plymouth reaches 78.71 per cent, Exeter 79.18 and Devonport 81.51.

'Devonport has 32 per cent of boys and 21 per cent of girls over Standard IV. In Plymouth only 19.7 per cent of the boys and 16.9 per cent of the girls are in similar standards. Forty three per cent of the Devon teachers are certificated, whilst in Cornwall only 34 per cent are certificated.' *(WMN 30 December 1899)*

'The Plymouth School Board have built handsome and commodious schools in several parts of the town and neighbourhood, amongst which may be mentioned those at Palace Court, Oxford Street, Mount Street, Wolsdon Street, How Street, Castle Street, Summerland Street, King Street, Treville Street and Sutton Road.' *(E 1898)*

'The sum obtained per head obtained in rates by the Board schools is 14s 8d in Devonport, 17s 8d in Plymouth, and £1 1s 1d in Exeter. The expenditure per head is £1 10s 8d in the voluntary schools of Devonport and £2 6s 1d in the Board schools: Plymouth £2 1s 2d.' *(WMN 30 December 1899)*

Another area where there have been great advances for children in the present century is that of literature with many author targeting that age group. Especially popular with boys have been adventure stories like those of Captain Marryat, with *Mr Midshipman Easy* and *Masterman Ready*, RM Ballantyne's *Coral Island* and Robert Louis Stevenson's *Treasure Island* and *Kidnapped*. For girls Charlotte Young's *The Daisy Chain* and *The Trial* have been very popular.

Children from class 9 of Union Street Infants School.

A wedding at St Andrew's Church

MARRIAGE

Across the last hundred years it would appear that the average age for a woman to marry is 18 while for a man it is more like 25. Queen Victoria herself was married in 1840 at the age of 20, the same age as her cousin and husband, Prince Albert.

Curiously enough when the Queen was born there were but a handful of parishes and consequently parish churches in the Three Towns, St Andrew's, the mother church, and Charles, in Plymouth, Stoke Damerel in Devonport and St George's in Stonehouse. Since that time the population has expanded so rapidly and so greatly that it has been necessary to create seven new sub-parishes from St Andrews — Christ Church, Eton Place, 1847; St James the Less, Citadel Road, 1847; St Peter 1847, Holy Trinity, Southside Street, 1854; St Saviour, Lambhay Hill, 1870; All Saints, Harwell Street, 1875 and St Michael, West Hoe, 1891. There have also been eight carved out of Stoke Damerel — St Paul, Morice Square, 1846; St Mary, James Street, 1846; St James the Great, Keyham Road, 1846; St Stephen, Mount Wise, 1846; St Michael, Albert Road, 1873; St Aubyn, Chapel Street, 1882 (the building dates from 1771); St Mark, Ford, 1885 and St John the Baptist, Duke Street, 1887 (again an older building). We have also seen four created out of Charles Parish — St John Sutton on Plym, 1855; Emmanuel, Mannamead, 1870; St Jude, Beaumont Road, 1876; and St Matthias, North Hill, 1887. There is also the addition of St Matthew in Clarence Street, as a new parish in Stonehouse.

The above serves to illustrate the comparative growth of the Three Towns: Plymouth's population at the beginning of the Nineteenth Century was 16,040, at the time of the 1891 census it was 85,610 — with more than 10,000 of those appearing in the last ten years. Devonport, by comparison has acquired an additional 6,000 residents in that same ten-year period and totalled 54,848 souls in 1891, while Stonehouse had grown but slightly from 15,125 to 15,398.

Two wedding groups and a pair of bridesmaids. The divorce rate, incidentally, is less than 1%.

Top left: *Hingston's Monumental Masons, 1894.* Top right: *Advert for J Walter Parson.* Bottom left: *A Naval funeral procession.* Bottom right: *Joseph Geach's premises off Cemetery Road, 1894.*

THE FINAL CHAPTER

It goes without saying that the more people we have living in the Three Towns, the more people we will have dying here too. Plymouth, Stonehouse and Devonport are currently blessed with over 70 firms offering their services as undertakers, among them some of the larger retailers in the area, and some of the leading furniture manufacturers like Popham, Radford & Co., Spooners, Westlake, Harding, Turpin and Parson.

The last named are among the oldest of them having been established by Richard Walter Parson, a carpenter and joiner from Stoke Climsland, in 1842. Back then the approximate cost of a funeral, or at least a polished elm coffin, a hearse, coach and cemetery fees, was around four pounds, by no means within the pocket of everyone. Neither are some of the more elaborate headstones on offer from various of the areas numerous monumental masons.

Not surprisingly many of these businesses are to be found around Pennycomequick, a stone's throw from the main burial ground for the Three Towns, particularly now that the graveyard for St Andrew's has been recently relocated and that of Charles Church has long since been constrained by the developments surrounding it.

'One of the leading concerns of its kind is that of Mr Joseph Geach. The proprietor's wide experience, including thirteen and a half years in one establishment and over six years in another, thoroughly qualifying him to run a business requiring for its success a technical training combined with energy and enterprise; and to these combinations must be attributed the measure of success that has attended his efforts as a monumental mason.

'Mr Geach's premises, conveniently situated in the Cemetery Road, comprise suitable buildings, abutting on the main thoroughfare, while in the rear are extensive works, equipped with the most improved appliances, and giving employment to upwards of sixteen thoroughly experienced hands.'

'A very fine stock of the best selected marble, Portland stone, and paints is held, and there is displayed a number of monuments, tablets, crosses, headstones, etc., all of the most artistic designs, and exhibiting most skilful workmanship; whilst in the cemeteries and churchyards in Plymouth and for miles around, may be seen beautiful examples of the work of this well-known house.' (W 1894)

In recent years, in some circles, the idea of cremation has been advanced. The issue was debated in The Lancet and the Queen's Physician, Sir Henry Thompson, is a keen advocate of the practice. Sir Henry feels that it would reduce the expense of furnerals, spare mourners the necessity of standing exposed to the weather during interment and further that urns would be safe from vandalism.

The Cremation Society of Great Britain was formed in 1874 and in 1885 a crematorium was established in Woking. By the end of the year three out of 597,357 deaths recorded in this country were cremations. On a happier note it is worth reflecting that during the course of the Nineteenth Century life expectancy in this country has increased from 40 to around 48 for men and from 42 to 52 for women ... although the maternal mortality rate is still a disconcerting figure fluctuating between 4% and 7%.

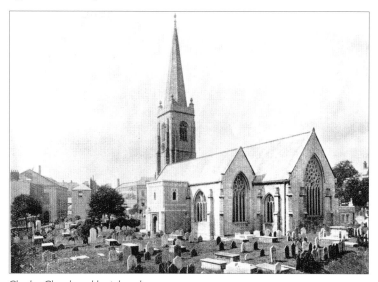

Charles Church and burial yard.

ACKNOWLEDGEMENTS

Firstly an enormous thank you to Steve Johnson, who allowed me free access to his wonderful collection of images — Stephen has been collecting and collating material for as long as, if not longer, than I have and his cyberheritage website is a great place for anyone interested in the history of this City to lose themselves for an hour or two, or three!

Special thanks also to Derek Tait, who has similarly allowed me the use of any of the many images he has pulled together over the years. Derek has produced an impressive number of Plymouth books over the years himself and is a great source of material and support.

Many years ago now Joan Dancer loaned me a dozen or so small photo albums taken and compiled by one of her Hawker ancestors in the 1880s and 1890s. Similarly, Winifred Hooper introduced me to a collection that her bicycling uncle, Walter Hooper, had put together around the same time. Among the other photographers whose work is featured here are Richard Rugg Monk and William Gilhen.

Ten years ago now I had a hand in setting up the Plymouth Barbican Trust's excellent South West Image Bank and this august body, under the direction firstly of Anna Keast, then Stacey Dyer and more recently Colette Hobbs — always with an excellent band of diligent and dedicated volunteers — has grown in stature and in depth.

Initially a repository of newspaper negatives from the last few decades of the Twentieth Century, it has grown into one of the principal picture repositories in the South West, covering almost all of that period that photography has been with us. As I write, SWIB is scheduled soon to join forces with the exciting new, and as yet unnamed Plymouth History Centre, bringing with it the tantalising prospect of having all of the City's major archives under one vast roof. What a great day in the story of Plymouth's history that promises to be.

Which is clearly an appropriate point to thank Plymouth City Art Gallery and Museum, and Plymouth Library Services who have been invaluable sources of information and material in recent months and years, as well as 25-30 years ago when I was putting together the first volume of words and pictures (exclusively drawings and engravings) dating back to the Victorian times.

Another well-thumbed source of information and imagery has been that well-loved, erstwhile must-have, local yearbook *Doidge's Annual*, a quirky source of printed matter that started life in the second half of the Nineteenth Century and was enjoying something of a golden age in the 1890s.

Old books, tourist guides, street directories, souvenir programmes and glossy brochures have also proved useful, as have the inevitable collections of old picture postcards.

By putting together a collection of over 600 images covering a 50-year-period it is hoped that a flavour of the fashions and the times will come across, especially with regard to clothing, hairstyles, and transport. There were no motor cars on our local roads, although here and there one might see an experimental steam-driven vehicle — and, as we have seen, the electric tram just managed to sneak in at the very end of Queen Victoria's reign.

However, while the Iron Horse was charging up and down the ever-expanding network of railways criss-crossing the country, the humble horse-and-cart was an integral part of everyday life, on the open road, in the town and in the country.

But if you are reading this there is every chance you will have already seen all that in the book, a book for which I still have a number of other thanks to make. From a practical and personal perspective, I'd like to express very grateful thanks to my long-suffering publisher and wife, Clare, my mother-in-law Patricia, New Street operations manager, Rob Warren, former Latimer Trend man Bill Bugler, Beverley Kinsella, and Mike and Anne Corry, all of whom have read this looking for typos, inaccuracies and inconsistencies.

Thanks too to successive *Herald* editors who I have worked for over the years: Jim Mitchell, Alan Goode, Alan Cooper, Alan Qualtrough, Rachel Campey, Ian Wood, Bill Martin and Paul Burton.

Walter Hooper - with bicycle ... and camera?

RN Worth

Henry Whitfeld

In terms of text, the internet, most notably via the wonderful British Newspaper Archive, Ancestry.com and, inevitably, Wikipedia has thrown up innumerable nuggets that have helped bring colour and detail to many of these pages.

Among the sources quoted are the *North Devon Journal* (NDJ), *The Star* (Guernsey: TSG), the *Illustrated London News* (ILN), the *Devon and Exeter Daily Gazette* (D&EDG), the *Banbury Advertiser* (BA), *Edinburgh Evening News* (EEN), *Western Times* (WT), *Irish Times* (IT), *Bradford Observer* (BO), *Worcester Journal* (WJ), *Royal Cornwall Gazette* (RCG), *Western Daily Mercury* (WDM), *Dundee Courier* (DC), *London Evening Standard* (LES), and *Western Figaro* (WF).

Among the principal sources used however the *Western Morning News* (WMN) is the main paper and WHK Wright's *Illustrated Handbook to Plymouth Stonehouse & Devonport* (Wright 1879) is the primary text. Wright also appears to have supplied the text to the *Plymouth Historical, Social and Commercial Guide* (Wright 1894) and most certainly the commentary for the *Streets of Old Plymouth* (Wright 1901), as well as a number of other books and papers and so is easily the largest single contributor to the text. RN Worth too, wrote extensively around that time and is also regularly quoted, as is his fellow Plymouth historian, Henry Whitfeld. Other sources include *The Strangers Handbook to Plymouth, Stonehouse and Devonport* (1851), the recollections of Samuel Weekes and *Plymouth As A Holiday Centre* (c1900).

Of course many of the images that appear in this book have been supplied by readers of my weekly column in the *Plymouth Herald* and the A-Z list below is to thank those who have sent me/loaned me photographs from this era over the last 25 years or so — photographs that have helped make this book what it is — I only hope I haven't left anyone out!

So thank you: Ron Andrews, Denise Bailey, Victor Barton, Guy Belshaw, David Buckingham, John and Sylvia Boulden, Tom Bowden, Arthur Clamp, Bob Cook, Andy Endacott, Marilyn Endacott, Guy Fleming, Michael Foot, Crispin Gill, Tom Greaves, Doreen Johnson, Alan Kittridge, William Henry Lawrence, Robert Leest, Edward Luscombe, Sally Luscombe, Audrey and Freddie Mills, Bob and Linda Mills, Brian Moseley, Sid Oliver, Ann Pallant, Joe Pengelly, Derry Purvis, Tom Savery, Stephen Smith, Alan Tibbitts, David Tozer, Fernely Wallis, Marshall Ware, and last but by no means least — Peter Waterhouse.

While every care has been taken to try and identify individual copyright holders the publishers would be happy to hear from anyone who has information concerning the copyright of any uncredited images.

Chris Robinson *October 2016*

BIBLIOGRAPHY

Around and About Plymouth and Devonport with a Camera – JW &S (c1900)

British Seaside Piers – **Chris Mawson and Richard Riding**, Ian Allan Publishing (2008)

Days in Devonport, Parts I-VII, **Gerald W Barker,** *ALC (1982-85)*

Devonshire, Historical, Descriptive, Biographical – **FJ Snell**, Mate & Sons, Ltd. (1907)

Devonshire: HIstorical and Pictorial - **J Sydney Curtis**, Topographical Publishing Co. (1899)

Doidge's Western Counties Illustrated Annual – (1888 -1901 inclusive)

Electricity in Plymouth: Its Origins and Development – **Edward W Luscombe**, The Devonshire Association (1999)

Eyre's *Plymouth, Devonport and Stonehouse District Directory* – Hammond Co., Ltd. London (1898)

Hoe, The – **Chatty Joe**, Doidge's Almanac, Plymouth (1882)

Images of England: Plymouth – **Derek Tait**, Tempus Publishing Ltd (2003)

Kelly's *Devonshire Directory*, also published by White and Billings – (1858-1919)

The Making of the University of Plymouth – **Alston Kennerley**, University of Plymouth (2000)

Mr Rawlinson's Report on the Sewerage, Drainage ... of Plymouth, PD&S Herald (1853)

Naval Heritage in The West: Part I, II & III – **Andy Endacott** (1986, 1987, 1988)

Old Plymouth, Streets of, – **C Eldred & WHK Wright** (1901)

100 Years of the Co-operative Society in Plymouth – **Chris Robinson,** Pen & Ink Publishing (2009)

Pictorial Plymouth, – **Robert K Dent**, JJ Allday (1900)

Playbill: A History of Theatre in the Westcountry – **Harvey Crane**, Macdonald and Evans Ltd (1980)

Plymouth – **RN Worth**, The Graphic (1878)

Plymouth, Book of Reference, **FE Sach**, FE Sach & Co. (1916)

Plymouth: A New History – **Crispin Gill**, Devon Books (1993)

Plymouth and District Illustrated Commercial Guide – **WHK Wright**, Plymouth (1894)

Plymouth and Devonport in Times of War and Peace – **H Whitfeld**, Plymouth (1900)

Plymouth and Devonport Guide with Sketches – **HE Carrington**, Byers & Son (1838)

Plymouth and Plymothians, More Photographs and Memories – **Andrew Cluer**, Lantern Book (1975)

 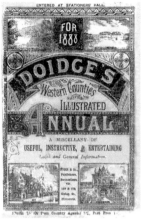  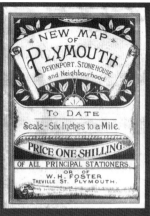 

Plymouth and Plymothians Photographs and Memories – **Andrew Cluer**, Lantern Books (1974)

Plymouth, As A Holiday Centre – **Henry Francis Whitfeld**, Plymouth Mercantile Association (1900)

Plymouth, History of – **RN Worth**, WIlliam Bredon & Son (1890)

Plymouth, History of – **John Harris**, typescript PLSL (1808)

Plymouth in the Late 'Forties, Person Recollections – **Samuel Weeks,** Brendon & Son, (1925)

Plymouth: Ocean Liner, Port of Call – **Alan Kittridge**, Twelveheads Press (1993)

Plymouth: Pictures from the Past – **Guy Fleming**, The Devonshire Press Ltd (1995)

Plymouth River: A History of the Laira and Cattewater – **Crispin Gill**, Devon Books (1997)

Plymouth, Stonehouse & Devonport Illustrated, Handbook – **WHK Wright**, WH Luke (1879)

Plymouth 100 Years of Street Travel – **RC Sambourne**, Glasney Press (circa 1970)

Plymouth's Electrical Revolution – **Edward Luscombe and Chris Buck**, South Western Electricity Historical Society (2014)

Plymouth's Historic Barbican – **Chris Robinson**, Pen & Ink Publishing (2007)

Plympton's Past in Pictures – **John Boulden** (2007)

Plympton St Maurice Guide – **Audrey Mills**, Plympton Civic Association (1981)

The Post Office Directory of Plymouth, Devonport, Stonehouse & District 1908, 1910-11 – Swiss & Co

Raglan Barracks – *Navy and Army Illustrated* (1896)

Rule Britannia, The Victorian World – **Perry & Mason** eds, Times Newspapers Ltd (1974)

Sherwell Story – **Stanley Griffin**, Plymouth (1964)

Showmen of the Past: Hancocks of the West – **Kevin Scrivens & Stephen Smith**, New Era Publications (2006)

St Budeaux,The Ancient Parish of – **Marshall Ware**, ALC (1983)

Sutton Harbour – **Crispin Gill**, Devon Books (1997)

The Trams of Plymouth: A 73-Year Story – **Martin Langley and Edwina Small**, Ex Libris Press (1990)

Victorian Plymouth: As Time Draws On – **Chris Robinson**, Pen & Ink Publishing (1991)

Whitelegg and Sons: Cavalcade of Shows – **Guy Belshaw**, New Era publications (2005)

Wolferstans, the First 200 Years – **Chris Robinson**, Pen & Ink (2012)

Dartmoor Hotel (left) and Queen Anne Terrace, North Hill, Tavistock Road c.1890

Chris Robinson's Plymouth

Local Books, Prints & DVDs

🐦 misterplymouth
www.chrisrobinson.co.uk

34 New Street
Barbican
Plymouth PL1 2NA
01752 228120